Slim and Healthy
Vegetarian

Slim and Healthy Vegetarian

JUDITH WILLS

Photography by Debbie Patterson

CRESCENT BOOKS
New York • Avenel

To Tony

Throughout the book recipes are for four people unless otherwise stated.

This 1995 edition is published by Crescent Books,
distributed by Random House Value Publishing, Inc.
40 Engelhard Avenue, Avenel, New Jersey 07001

Random House
New York · Toronto · London · Sydney · Auckland

The publishers would like to thank Michael Gilbert & Raymond,
Madame Renée Mason, and the inhabitants of Couddes in France's Loire
Valley for their help in the location photography.

Editorial Direction Lewis Esson Publishing
American Editor Norma MacMillan
Art Direction Mary Evans
Design Alison Fenton
Design Assistant Ian Muggeridge
Photography and Styling Debbie Patterson
Illustrations Lynne Robinson
Food Styling Jane Suthering
Editorial Assistant Penny David
Production Controller Clare Coles

A CIP catalog record for this book is available from the Library of Congress.

ISBN 0-517-14236-8

Typesetting by Ian Muggeridge, London
Printed and bound in Singapore
8 7 6 5 4 3 2 1

CONTENTS

Vegetarian eating for health

Here we look at the constituents of a vegetarian diet and discover just why well-balanced vegetarian eating can be so healthy.

Doesn't it seem such a very long time ago that vegetarians were thought of as a cranky minority, to be viewed with suspicion and offered – *always* – a cheese omelet if we ever inadvertently let one near our supper tables?

Today, even if we're not vegetarian – or semi-vegetarian – ourselves, we almost all have at least one vegetarian in the family, and we all have several vegetarian friends. Furthermore, the number of non-meat eaters is growing daily, as more and more people discover the health benefits of a diet based around grains, fruit and vegetables.

There are also a growing number of vegetarian cookbooks on the shelves. Sadly, many of them are still caught in the trap of too much *worthiness* and too little variety and taste. Others don't do vegetarianism any favor by including far too many recipes full of fats, oils, and high-fat dairy products. Surely one of the main reasons that people turn to vegetarian eating is that it is – or should be – a *healthy* way to eat, as well as a compassionate one.

So it is for people who are still seeking healthy yet tasty, light yet satisfying, wide-ranging yet simple – and above all easy, or fairly easy and quick-to-prepare – meals that I have researched *Slim and Healthy Vegetarian*.

Within these pages I hope that you will find a collection of meals to suit you and your lifestyle as well as your body. I hope also that you will appreciate the first two chapters containing all the basic information the new vegetarian (or part-time vegetarian) needs to ensure a balanced, appealing diet.

You will also, I hope, be pleased to see – as you flick through the menus and recipes – that, within the limits of vegetarianism itself, there are no "banned" foods at all. Certain high-fat, low-nutrient foods may be limited, for sure, but you will see you can incorporate fabulous cakes, cookies and desserts into a healthy diet, as well as cheeses, cream, and oils.

The secret of any good diet is balance and taste. That is what *Slim and Healthy Vegetarian* is all about. Enjoy it – and remember that enjoyment is twice as sweet when there is no guilt attached!

WHAT IS A VEGETARIAN?

There are several different "degrees" of vegetarianism and, if you are new to the subject or are unsure about catering for a vegetarian, it is important to clarify the differences right away. In fact, if you are cooking for any vegetarian, always ask them *exactly* what they don't eat to avoid any embarrassment at serving time.

SEMI-VEGETARIANS aren't true vegetarians, but I include a description here as many people who call themselves "vegetarians" are, in fact, "semis." Normally, semi-vegetarians can be described as people who don't eat any red meat, but will eat poultry and fish from time to time. However, some semi-vegetarians eat no poultry either, just fish.

Also, some people who call themselves semi-vegetarians *do* eat red meat occasionally – they will, say, eat it if there is nothing else offered at a dinner party but would not eat it at home. So if someone says they are "semi-veg," it is important to inquire further!

VEGETARIANS can be divided into two sub-groups:

Lacto-ovo-vegetarians eat no flesh of any kind – no meat, poultry, or fish. They *do* eat eggs and all dairy products, including cheese, milk, yogurt, and butter.

Lacto-vegetarians eat everything lacto-ovo-vegetarians eat except eggs.

So, again – when catering for vegetarians it is important to know whether they will or won't eat eggs.

VEGANS go further than vegetarians, eating no flesh, no eggs, and no dairy products of any kind. Some vegans will eat honey, others won't. Some avoid any connection with what they consider cruelty to animals by not wearing leather or fur, and not using cosmetics or other products tested on animals. They eat nothing but plant foods.

FRUITARIANS are even stricter than vegans, eating only fruits, nuts, and seeds. The fruitarian diet is very restricted and beyond the scope of this book.

Apart from fruitarians, all other types of true vegetarian will find recipes to suit them in the following chapters – although, as most vegetarians are lacto-ovo-vegetarians, the majority of recipes are more suitable for them.

If you are vegetarian, or thinking of going vegetarian, it is up to you to decide what you will and won't eat – and why. Many people give up eating flesh on moral or compassionate grounds, but perhaps the biggest reason people make the change to vegetarianism is that they hope it will improve their health and well-being – and perhaps it will help to keep them slim.

HOW HEALTHY IS A VEGETARIAN DIET?

Indeed, if you follow a well-balanced vegetarian diet, all the research to date appears to confirm that you will be eating healthily. Here's why:

* It should be lower in saturated fats (found mainly in meat and dairy products) and in fats in general than an average carnivorous diet – particularly veganism.

* It should be high in complex carbohydrates. These are the unrefined or low-refined starchy foods that should form the majority of the average vegetarian diet – bread, rice and other grains, pasta, potatoes, cereals, dried beans, peas, and lentils, and fresh fruits and vegetables. These complex carbohydrates provide bulk for the diet and plenty of fiber and most also provide good amounts of protein. This makes for a diet high in benefits, including less risk of heart disease and certain forms of cancer, less digestive disorders, obesity, and diabetes. (Oats and legumes, in particular, appear to have an especially beneficial effect on blood cholesterol levels.)

* It should be high in vitamins, especially the antioxidant vitamins beta-carotene, C, and E. Beta-carotene is a "pro-form" of vitamin A (i.e. the body converts it to vitamin A) and it is found in many brightly colored vegetables and fruits. These antioxidant vitamins appear to offer protection against heart disease and cancers. Optimum vitamin intake also has many other health benefits.

* It should be low in refined products and products high in additives.

* It should help us to stay slim. A reduced-fat diet, high in complex carbohydrates, naturally limits overall calorie intake by helping us to feel full both during and after eating and by providing plenty of "bulk" on the plate.

No wonder, then, that vegetarians have:

* On average, a 20% lower blood-cholesterol level than meat-eaters.

* A 30% lower cancer rate than meat-eaters.
* Less incidence than meat-eaters of all the following: heart disease, kidney stones, osteoporosis, diabetes, diverticulitis, hemorrhoids, angina, gout, dental decay, and rheumatoid arthritis.

The fact is that a well-balanced vegetarian diet consisting of a high proportion of fresh fruit and vegetables and starchy foods is almost the exact recipe for healthy eating as prescribed by the World Health Organization (W.H.O.) in 1990.

GETTING IT RIGHT

However, not everyone who goes vegetarian does eat such a well-balanced diet, low in fat and high in complex carbohydrates and vitamins. Here are some ways in which a vegetarian diet may not be as healthy as it could be:

* Some people just give up meat, poultry, and fish and simply carry on eating the rest of their diet as before – e.g. a main meal of roasted potatoes and vegetables but no meat, or fish and chips without the fish! Such a diet is likely to be short of both protein and calories, and is likely to make the new vegetarian hungry and quickly bored with "vegetarian" eating.

* Some people give up flesh and simply replace it by eating extra cheese and eggs. There is nothing wrong with cheese and eggs in small amounts – especially lowfat cheese, but many types of cheese contain a great deal of saturated fat. Traditional Cheddar, for example, contains three-quarters of its calories as fat calories. Even eggs are 67% fat and only 33% protein. And in 100 calories' worth of whole milk, 52 of them are fat calories! So just by giving up meat, poultry, and fish, it doesn't necessarily mean vegetarians will be cutting down on fat if instead they choose high-fat dairy products as protein sources.

* Many vegetarians carry on eating a high-fat diet because they eat a lot of butter or margarine on bread, or use oil in cooking. They often eat a lot of pastry – most of which is very high in fat – and baked goods. Many also eat lots of fat in the form of cakes, desserts, cookies, and candy – perhaps thinking that because they are cutting down on animal products, they don't need to feel guilty about indulging their sweet tooth.

* People who are vegan may also have problems – if they are not careful, they may fall short on various nutrients, particularly iron, protein, calcium, and vitamin B12.

However, all these potential problems are not difficult to overcome with a little know-how. There is no need to turn yourself into a walking nutrition manual, though. All you need is a little time to learn the basics, and then you can easily build a balanced and pleasant vegetarian diet.

THE NUTRIENTS WE NEED

All the food that we eat provides us with calories (i.e. energy). The calories in our food can be calories from carbohydrate, calories from fat, or calories from protein. If we get the right balance of those three energy-giving foods, we should also get a good balance of the other things we need for good health – vitamins, minerals, trace elements, and fiber. (Of course, it goes without saying that we also need water.)

An average female diet to maintain a reasonable body weight contains about 2,000 calories a day; for men the figure is around 2,700. For optimum health, according to World Health Organization recommendations, we should aim to eat no more than 30% of those calories as fat; we should eat at least 55% of those calories as carbohydrate; and 10%–15% of them should be protein.

For practical purposes, there is no such thing as a food that is purely carbohydrate (except sugar) or purely fat (except oil) or purely protein – most are a mix of at least two of those elements. Nevertheless, foods can be grouped as predominantly carbohydrate foods and predominantly fat foods. The best protein sources in a vegetarian diet tend to be from lowfat, high-carbohydrate foods. Very few vegetarian foods are predominantly protein.

CARBOHYDRATES

These are the starchy and sugary foods.

The complex carbohydrates as mentioned above are the unrefined plant foods of all types. We include all fruits and vegetables in this group because, although many fruits and vegetables are quite low in starch, they add bulk and fiber to the diet. All of these complex carbohydrates – with the exception of most fruits – also contain good or very good amounts of lowfat protein.

Legumes – all peas, beans, and lentils – deserve a special mention because not only are they a very lowfat food, they also contain more protein than the other complex carbohydrate foods – around 30%.

Fruits and vegetables are a vitally important part of your diet; as well as providing plenty of bulk, fiber, and color to your plate for few calories, they are also one of the vegetarian's most important sources of vitamins and minerals.

The sugary or "simple" carbohydrates are sugars, syrups, honey, glucose – these types of carbohydrates contain no fiber and few if any vitamins and minerals. According to the W.H.O., they should form no more than 10% of your total calorie intake (within the 55% already mentioned for total carbohydrate intake).

So, obviously, as complex carbohydrate calories should make up around half of your daily diet, it is important that you include several from this group in your diet each day and at each meal.

FATS

There are three types of fat in our diet: saturated, monounsaturated, and polyunsaturated.

Saturated fat is the type mostly found in red meat and dairy products. Because of the apparent link between a high-saturated-fat diet and heart disease, some cancers, obesity, and other health problems, the W.H.O. suggests that we should limit our saturated fat intake to 10% of total calories and a third of total fat intake. That is why it is important on a vegetarian diet not to rely too heavily on dairy products for your protein unless they are mostly low-fat dairy products.

Most fatty foods contain at least some monounsaturated fats, but both olive oil and peanut oil are particularly high in them. Monounsaturated fat is not linked with heart disease and it could, indeed, have a beneficial effect on the cardiovascular system. Around 10% of your day's total calories could come from this type of monounsaturated fat.

Polyunsaturated fats are, again, present to some degree in most fatty foods, but found in largest quantities in sunflower, corn, canola, and safflower oils. Polyunsaturates can reduce blood-cholesterol levels, and we should aim to consume, again, 10% of our daily calories as polyunsaturates – bringing our total daily fat intake to 30%. Less fat than this certainly wouldn't do us any harm – especially those trying to lose weight.

A diet high in plant foods will naturally ensure that the balance of the three types of fat is kept at a reasonable level. So as long as you take care not to consume too much of the high-fat vegetarian foods you shouldn't have a problem with too much fat in your diet.

HIGH-FAT VEGETARIAN FOODS TO EAT IN SMALL OR MODERATE AMOUNTS:

* All cheeses, except those specifically marked "lowfat" (even half-fat cheeses contain quite a lot of fat).
* Whole milk – choose lowfat or skim, or soy milk instead.
* Cream, all kinds – choose non-dairy lowfat cream substitute instead or plain yogurt.
* Butter – choose lowfat spread instead.
* Eggs: although a good source of protein and vitamins, consumption is best restricted to three or four a week.
* Nuts: all nuts, except chestnuts, are very high in fat, with moderate amounts of protein, so if you are watching your weight they are best used in small quantities within other dishes or as a special treat.
* Seeds: as nuts.
* Coconut meat and cream: high in saturated fat, so use with caution!
* Pastry – choose phyllo, which allows you to control the amount and type of fat that you brush on it.
* Desserts, candies, and baked goods: experiment with lower-fat, lower-sugar recipes, such as the ones on pages 106–17. Grated carrot or sweet potato or mashed banana can all be added to give bulk, "mouth feel," texture, and sweetness rather than using lots of fat and sugar.
* Cooking oils and salad oils: just go easy on these – most recipes use far more oil than is necessary.

Experiment to see how much you can cut down, as I have done in the recipes in this book. Add flavor with calorie-free herbs and spices.

PROTEIN

Protein is the material with which we build and repair new body tissue. Adults need around 10%–15% of their daily calories to be protein and, in fact, most meat-eaters get much more than this.

New vegetarians often worry about whether or not they will get enough protein in their diet – especially if they don't want to eat too many dairy products (traditionally a good source of protein after flesh foods). As protein is contained in such a wide range of plant foods, however, if you eat a varied diet containing enough calories overall it is highly unlikely that you would suffer a protein shortage, even if you eat no dairy products at all.

Why then, for so long, was vegetable protein thought of as "second class" protein? Well, protein is made up of

20 different amino acids. Eight of these amino acids are called "essential," because the body can't synthesize them itself and so they must be provided in our food. Meat and animal products contain these eight essential amino acids in one "package," whereas most vegetable sources of protein contain some, but not all. For example, lentils are high in the amino acid lysine, while rice is low in lysine but higher in the other seven. So if you eat, say, rice and lentils at the same meal, you will be getting a "complete" protein meal with everything you need supplied by the two different plant products.

Until recently it was thought that for vegetarians to obtain enough "complete" protein from their diet, they would have to combine the different types of plant protein at each meal. The newest thinking says that as long as you have a varied and well-balanced diet on a daily basis, it isn't absolutely essential always to eat "complementary" proteins at each meal.

However, as the complementary proteins theory is really quite simple, it is worth listing the combinations of plant foods here that *will* give you complete protein within one meal:

1 Grains (rice, rye, wheat, barley, millet, corn, buckwheat, etc.) with a legume (lentils, beans of any kind, peas). Some examples: beans on toast, rice and bean salad, hummus with pita, lentil pâté with crispbread, split pea soup with rolls.

2 Legumes with nuts or seeds. Some examples: chickpea and sesame seed salad, cashew dip with crudités followed by lentil soup.

3 Any plant protein with milk, milk products, and eggs. This means the protein quality of any plant food can be enhanced by the addition of a little lowfat dairy product. Some examples: potatoes contain good amounts of protein which can be made complete with the addition of a lowfat cheese sauce; rice can be enhanced by adding skim milk for a rice pudding.

As you can see, most of the time we practice this "protein complementing" without even thinking about it, because the combinations of foods seem natural.

All the main meal, supper, and main-course salad recipes in this book will give you "complete protein" – and, if you add bread of some kind to your soups, dips, spreads, and appetizers, you will also get complete protein from most of them.

However, do remember that as long as you get a good variety of food on a daily basis, you don't really need to worry too much about this protein combining, and most plant foods – with the exception of fruit – contain good amounts of protein. Incidentally, soybeans in all their forms are the best source of lowfat protein.

Here are some other good sources:

* Soy flour, tofu, textured vegetable protein (T.V.P.), myco-protein ("Quorn"), chickpeas, lentils, dried beans of all kinds, split peas, brown rice, rye, oatmeal, wheat and wheatgerm, millet, corn, barley, pasta, potatoes.

* Nuts and seeds are a good source, but have a high fat content (around 70%) and so are high in calories.

* Leafy green vegetables also contain good amounts of protein although, as they are high-bulk low-calorie foods, it would be hard to get enough protein from them alone.

VITAMINS, MINERALS, AND FIBER

Vegetarians who get adequate calories and complex carbohydrates, fruit and vegetables are highly unlikely to need to worry about whether or not they are getting adequate vitamins and minerals in their diet.

All foods – apart from simple sugars – contain trace elements, and all plant food contains fiber. The proportions and amounts vary from food to food – for instance, oranges are a good source of vitamin C but contain low amounts of most of the B vitamins; while peanuts are a good source of vitamin E, but contain no vitamin C at all.

So, again, as long as you eat a varied diet you should get a good cross section of vitamins and minerals.

For interest and easy reference I have listed below the main sources in a vegetarian diet of all the most important vitamins and minerals, plus the best sources of fiber (for your guidance they are listed within each section in order of richness). Also, all the recipes in the book have a nutrition panel containing vitamin and mineral information.

VITAMIN A (retinol) – important for good vision.
Best sources: all dairy products.

BETA-CAROTENE (can be converted to vitamin A in the body) – antioxidant vitamin thought to offer protection against heart disease and cancers.
Best sources: carrots, parsley, red chili peppers, kale, spinach, dark green leaves of all kinds, sweet potatoes, apricots, nectarines, watercress, tomato paste, broccoli, grape leaves, fennel, cantaloupe, peaches, leeks, squash, mango, prunes, tomatoes, asparagus, peas, corn.

VITAMIN B group (consists of six different B vitamins, usually grouped together because they often occur in the same type of food) – important mainly for maintaining a healthy nervous system and converting food into energy.

VITAMIN B1 (thiamine)

Best sources: brewers' yeast, sunflower seeds, millet, yeast extract, wheatgerm, cilantro leaves, soybeans, alfalfa sprouts, Brazil nuts, wholewheat spaghetti, peanuts, sesame seeds, adzuki beans, split peas, millet, rolled oats, black-eyed peas, kidney beans, chickpeas, lentils, other nuts and legumes.

VITAMIN B2 (riboflavin)

Best sources: yeast extract, brewers' yeast, Chinese mushrooms, almonds, wheatgerm, Camembert and Danish Blue cheeses, alfalfa, egg yolk, adzuki beans, Cheddar, Parmesan, and Edam cheeses, mushrooms, soybeans, broccoli, yogurt, black-eyed peas, other nuts and legumes.

VITAMIN B3 (niacin)

Best sources: yeast extract, brewers' yeast, peanuts, Chinese mushrooms, soybeans, wholewheat spaghetti, wheatgerm, Parmesan cheese, barley, black-eyed peas, brown rice, split peas, wheat, lentils, lima beans, wholewheat bread.

VITAMIN B6 (pyridoxine)

Best sources: wheatgerm, soybeans, oats, walnuts, lentils, lima beans, navy beans, barley, hazelnuts, bananas, mung beans, peanuts, kidney beans, avocados, white rice, raisins, Brussels sprouts, kale, leeks, potatoes, prunes, sweet potato, broccoli, red cabbage, Camembert cheese.

VITAMIN B12 (cobalamin)

Best sources: egg yolk, hard and cottage cheeses, yeast extract, milk, fortified soy milk, edible seaweed.

IMPORTANT NOTE: Vegans should take special care to get enough vitamin B12 in their diets.

FOLIC ACID

Best sources: yeast extract, black-eyed peas, wheatgerm, endive, brewers' yeast, chickpeas, mung beans, broccoli, kidney beans, spinach, Brussels sprouts, lima beans, peanuts, hearty greens, okra, soybeans, almonds, beets, cabbage, Napa cabbage, peas, hazelnuts, parsnips, avocado, walnuts, Camembert, oatmeal, string beans, sweet potato, corn, other whole grains and legumes.

VITAMIN C (ascorbic acid) – important for healthy tissues and the absorption of minerals: the antioxidant vitamin. Heat and light will destroy it.

Best sources: guavas, chili peppers, sweet peppers, black currants, parsley, kale, sorrel, broccoli, tomato paste, Brussels sprouts, lemons, cauliflower, cabbage, strawberries, watercress, red cabbage, spinach, oranges, limes, gooseberries, grapefruit, lychees, mango, beansprouts, new potatoes, hearty greens, tangerines, melon, okra, peas, pineapple, raspberries, rutabaga, sweet potato, all other fresh fruit and vegetables.

VITAMIN D (cholecalciferol) – important for the body's absorption of calcium.

Best sources: can be manufactured by the body in sunlight; otherwise found in fortified margarines and dairy products.

VITAMIN E (tocopherols) – important for healthy skin and cells and also an important antioxidant.

Best sources: wheatgerm oil, sunflower oil, safflower oil, palm oil, sunflower margarines, wheatgerm, hazelnuts, almonds, pecans, canola oil, peanut oil, corn oil, soybean oil, peanuts, green cabbage, Brazil nuts, olive oil, sweet potatoes, avocados, asparagus, butter, spinach, oatmeal, eggs, wholewheat flour, broccoli, tomatoes, hearty greens, Brussels sprouts, black currants, Parmesan cheese, barley, soybeans, brown rice.

IRON – needed for healthy blood; absorption improved by eating vitamin C at same meal.

Best sources: dulse (sea vegetable), curry powder, pistachios, alfalfa, Chinese mushrooms, adzuki beans, wheatgerm, soybeans, mung beans, sesame seeds, lentils, soy flour, dried peaches and apricots, millet, navy beans, black-eyed peas, chickpeas, egg yolk, barley, lima beans, split peas, tofu, bulghur, green spinach pasta, soy sauce, Brazil nuts, fava beans, oatmeal, wholewheat flour, cashew nuts, white pasta, wholewheat bread.

CALCIUM – needed for healthy bones and teeth and correct functioning of cardiovascular system.

Best sources: edible seaweed, Parmesan, Cheddar, and Edam, molasses, tofu, grape leaves, Feta and Camembert, dried figs, almonds, kale, soybeans, Brazil nuts, yogurt, navy beans, Napa cabbage, chickpeas, kidney beans, sesame seeds, egg yolk, milk, muesli, black-eyed peas, fava beans, broccoli, mung beans, rhubarb, lowfat soft cheeses, currants, spinach, dried apricots, hearty greens, lima beans, adzuki beans, Chinese mushrooms, okra.

ZINC – needed for the correct functioning of the healing processes and enzyme activity.

Best sources: wheatgerm, sesame seeds, yeast, alfalfa, sunflower seeds, oats, Brazil nuts, curry powder, Cheddar, Edam, and Parmesan cheeses, split peas, adzuki beans, egg yolk, barley, almonds, lentils, Camembert cheese, walnuts, peanuts, rye, wholewheat flour, wholewheat bread, other legumes.

POTASSIUM – needed for cellular activity.

Best sources: edible seaweed, molasses, dried apricots, lima beans, soybeans, soy flour, navy beans, dates, currants, peanut butter, walnuts, black-eyed peas, lentils, potatoes, barley, mushrooms, spinach, coconut, corn on the cob, pasta, rye, avocados, banana, sweet potato.

FIBER

Best sources: dried apricots, dried figs, prunes, dried peaches, almonds, soy and wholewheat flour, dried beans of all kind, lentils of all kinds, split peas, chickpeas, oatmeal, raspberries.

Notes: Raw wheat-bran is high in fiber but shouldn't be relied upon as a regular fiber source because it can prevent the body absorbing certain minerals that are eaten at the same time.

All the other trace elements not mentioned here will be supplied in a diet rich in the above vitamins.

GOING VEGETARIAN?

In the next two chapters you will get plenty of advice and practical tips on stocking up your pantry and on menu-planning, but if you are still simply thinking of going vegetarian the best advice both for practical purposes and for bodily acclimatization is to do so gradually.

People who come off a typical Western high-fat, low-fiber diet onto suddenly large amounts of lentils, beans, vegetables, and grains often find their digestive systems protesting – hardly surprising. The same would be true of vegetarians suddenly giving up their diet and going on a high-meat, low-fiber diet!

So give your body a chance to adapt and give yourself a chance to get used to different ways of shopping, meal-planning, and cooking by making the process of conversion a gradual one.

Here are some ways you could make the gradual change:

1   Replace meat, poultry, and fish meals twice a week for two weeks. Then increase this to three times a week for two weeks, and so on, until you have eliminated flesh altogether. Meanwhile, busy yourself building up a collection of meals that you enjoy.

2   Cut down portion sizes of flesh products on your plate and increase portion sizes of plant foods. Aim to replace the flesh products with the high-protein plant foods such as legumes, and try not to rely too much on dairy products.

The easiest way to alter the balance on your plate is to create "composite" dishes – e.g. pilaffs, risotti, curries, paellas, mixed salads, stir-fries, etc. You can also, if you like, use vegetable protein (e.g. soy chunks or vegetarian mince) as a meat substitute until you get more used to basic vegetarian cooking.

3   First cut out red meat for a few weeks. Replace it with high-protein vegetarian foods as above, then cut out poultry for another few weeks, again replacing that with vegetarian dishes, not simply more fish. Finally, cut out fish too, replacing that with more vegetarian dishes.

A VEGETARIAN IN THE FAMILY

Shopping and cooking for a lone vegetarian can seem a daunting proposition but it isn't really. Here are some ideas to help you:

*   Enjoy eating with the vegetarian at least a couple of times a week – why cook those delicious meals if you don't enjoy them yourself at least some of the time?

*   Once or twice a week, make similar meals to those you are making for the non-vegetarians in the family, but use vegetarian protein instead – e.g. a meat loaf using textured vegetable protein, a tofu and mushroom quiche instead of chicken and mushroom, a tofu stir-fry instead of a beef one. Whenever you are making non-vegetarian casseroles, quiches, and so on, make an individual container with a vegetarian filling for the vegetarian – or freeze it for later.

*   Don't feel guilty about using vegetarian "fast foods" to create quick and easy meals for one – pasta, rice, pita breads, salads, and vegetable stir-fries are all nutritious and tasty.

*   Batch-cook and freeze a selection of the soups, sauces, and dips from the appropriate chapters in this book. You can then easily create instant meals. (For more advice, read "Short Cuts to Good Food" on page 29.)

So now let's turn all this advice on nutrition into practical reality. The next chapter will show you how to build up a really workable and interesting vegetarian pantry.

The vegetarian kitchen

Planning a delicious and nutritious vegetarian diet is made much easier with the help of a well-stocked pantry. Here you'll find all the information you will need about buying, storing, and preparing every type of vegetarian food.

Every vegetarian cook shou d aim to build up a comprehensive stock of basic – and more exotic – items. You'll then find that, with the addition of a very few fresh ingredients or side dishes, you'll never be at a loss for a quick and easy – or even a more elaborate – meal.

This chapter guides you through the contents of the ideal pantry, refrigerator, and freezer; with tips on buying, storing, shelf-life, and preparation. f you're a new vegetarian, starting to cook for a vegetarian, or perhaps a long-term vegetarian who has slipped into lazy ways, you'll find the information here invaluable. Having a well-stocked pantry will help you to avoid the trap that so many vegetarians fall into – boring, monotonous meals and incomplete nutrition. However busy or inexperienced you are, you need not resign yourself to that. In fact, I've devoted a special section to the busy cook (and who isn't busy these days, at least some of the time?). You'll see that, with very little planning, your shopping and cooking can be made quick and easy.

Once you know *what* to buy, *where* to buy is no longer a problem for vegetarians. At last, a variety of good-quality items is not hard to find. Whereas no more than 10 years ago you would find it hard to obtain more than one or two different kinds of, say, dried bean at the local supermarket and hardly any more at the health-food store, you can now easily find ten or more varieties at the supermarket alone. Supermarkets are also a good place to seek out specialty oils and vinegars, cheese, pasta, and grains.

Your local health-focd store is well worth browsing around, for most have the widest selection of grains, dried fruits, spices, and nuts – also at lower cost. Your specialty grocer is bound to be a good source of bottles jars, and cans of more exotic items, and also of unusual breads.

Lastly, the chapter looks at fresh fruit and vegetables, with a guide to the more exotic varieties and important advice on buying and storing. The recent wide availability of good vegetarian, foodstuffs is all thanks to the growing demand from the ever-increasing army of vegetarians, part-time vegetarians, and semi-vegetarians. If you can't find what you're looking for in your local store, do ask. Many stores will stock items specially for you.

One great bonus of vegetarian food is that most of the basics are inexpensive – so there is no need to feel at all guilty when you purchase those luxury items. Shopping for your vegetarian meals – and cooking to fill up the freezer when you have the time – are two very enjoyable pastimes, so don't be afraid to buy and don't be afraid to experiment.

GRAINS

If grains mean little more to you than long-grain rice or rolled oats, here's where your thinking starts to change! Grains of many kinds are a staple part of the vegetarian diet – and a delicious one, too! Grains are almost perfect food – high in carbohydrate, low in fat, and containing good amounts of protein, vitamins, and minerals – so use them as often as you can. Start off with two or three kinds and gradually try out more as you get more confident.

Store grains in airtight containers in cool, dry conditions, and use within one year for whole grains or three months for rolled or flaked grains and flours.

You will find some of the grains described here in your supermarket; for others you may have to visit your health-food shop, but try to ensure it is a health-food shop with a rapid turnover so that your grains aren't likely to be stale when you buy them.

BARLEY

The kind of barley you want to buy is "pot" barley rather than "pearl" barley, the latter having been milled out of much of its goodness. Pot barley is a good addition to soups and casseroles and can be served as a grain on its own. It does have a long cooking time, however – up to two hours!

BUCKWHEAT

High in nutrients, it is particularly popular in Russia. The grains can be boiled like rice or ground into buckwheat flour, which is particularly good mixed with equal parts of wholewheat flour for pancakes.

BULGHUR

This is the name for wheat that has gone through a process of steaming, drying, and crushing so that it simply needs soaking to make it ready to eat or, occasionally, a little further boiling or steaming. Bulghur makes a nice change from rice and is probably best known for its use in the Mediterranean herb salad, *tabbouleh*.

CORN

Buy some corn kernels to make homemade popcorn (it's easy – just add a layer to a little oil in a heavy, lidded pan and heat until you hear the popping!).

Fine cornmeal makes polenta – a delicious supper dish (see page 74) – and you can also use cornmeal to make tortillas, cornbread, and many other dishes.

COUSCOUS

Yet another form of wheat, it is tiny bits of semolina. The precooked form needs only soaking to be ready to eat (it can be soaked in stock for more flavor). Widely used in North Africa, it is good with beans as a vegetable stuffing.

MILLET

This golden grain is high in iron. Try stir-frying the whole grains in a little oil, then boiling them like rice until soft.

OATS

These are particularly good at staving off hunger pangs and are rich in nutrients. Rolled oats are used for oatmeal cereal, muesli, and oatcakes (see page 114), and can also be used as a topping for casseroles and fruit crisps.

You can also use oat flour mixed with wheat flour for a tasty bread. Use oat flour up quickly as its high oil content can make it go rancid quite readily.

RICE

Brown rice is the whole grain and contains the most vitamin B. It takes around 40 minutes to boil and has a good nutty flavor and bite to it.

White rice comes in many varieties. There is nothing wrong with the ordinary *long-grain rice* that you can buy everywhere (look at the pack to ensure you are not buying a bag containing a lot of broken rice grains – a sign of poor quality). It contains less fiber and vitamins than brown rice, but that may not matter in a varied diet. Of the long-grain white rices, my favorite is Basmati rice, for good flavor and easy cooking, especially to accompany Indian dishes and in paellas. For use in Asian dishes, *Thai fragrant rice* (Jasmine rice) is better, producing a classic, softer texture. *Arborio rice* is perhaps the best-known of the Italian rices for risotto – it is short-grained and absorbs more liquid than long-grain rice.

Short-grain rice, with its fat, round grains, has a high starch content, which makes it very suitable for rice puddings.

Wild rice is not really a rice at all but looks like it. It is an expensive black, or near-black, grain that can take quite a time to cook, but it will add flavor, color, and interest to rice dishes and salads. It is usually not served on its own, but is mixed in small proportions with other rice – possibly because of its costliness.

RYE

This strong-flavored grain can be cracked and boiled like rice; rye flour can be used with wheat flour to make a robust bread. The cooked grains can also be used in many savory dishes.

WHEAT

The major source of carbohydrate in our Western diets.

Cracked wheat can be cooked like rice. Wheat flakes can be added to muesli or crumble toppings.

Wheat flour is, of course, used for bread, cakes, and pastries, as well as pasta (see below). It is best to use wholewheat flour as it is more nutritious, but refined white flour is a good source of calcium and you shouldn't refuse to eat it now and then!

The outer part of the wheat grain when milled is called *bran* and is high in fiber: do not, however, sprinkle it on everything as it can impede absorption of minerals. The inner part of the wheat grain is *wheatgerm*, which is a valuable addition to breakfast cereals, or may be sprinkled in drinks or on fruit or added to bread.

See also bulghur and couscous.

PASTA

You can make your own pasta even without any special equipment (see page 120), or you can buy a pasta machine and make a variety of shapes.

Pasta is basically a mixture of wheat flour (hard durum wheat is best) and water, with or without eggs. Vegans should note that pasta purchased in fresh form usually contains eggs, whereas dried pasta usually does not.

Whole-grain pasta contains more fiber and B vitamins than white or colored pasta; nevertheless, white pasta is still a good source of carbohydrate and protein.

If you buy your pasta dried, stock up your pantry with three or four different kinds. Pasta keeps well and, as you experiment, you will find that different types and shapes are best for different uses. Stock up on the following, and you should be prepared for every eventuality:

Lasagne sheets: plain, wholewheat, or green (with spinach). For baked lasagne, or can be rolled into cannelloni tubes.

Macaroni: good with cheese sauce or in casseroles.

Shells (small): good for salads and heavy sauces.

Shells (large): good for filling with a savory mixture and serving as a first course.

Flat pasta (e.g. *fettuccine*): good with creamy sauces and pesto.

Long, thin pasta (e.g. *spaghetti, spaghettini*): good with thin sauces that contain no large pieces (e.g. tomato). (The colored pastas simply make the plate look nicer, especially if you have a non-colorful sauce.)

Note: all pasta should be cooked only until "al dente," i.e. still a little firm to the bite.

ASIAN NOODLES

Asian Noodles are similar to pasta in many ways – a mixture of flour and water, sometimes with egg. Here are a few you may consider adding to your pantry, as they are so versatile, and easy and quick to prepare:

Egg-thread noodles (medium or fine): used in Chinese cooking, they are ready to soak and eat; only suitable for lacto-ovo-vegetarians.

Rice noodles: thin and white, these are made from rice flour; suitable for vegans.

Cellophane noodles: fine translucent noodles made from mung-bean flour and water; suitable for vegans.

LEGUMES

Legumes include beans, peas, and lentils, and their dried seeds (called pulses) are the major source of protein in the vegetarian diet. Most have to be soaked before cooking, although you can buy most kinds precooked and canned if you only want a small quantity. It is always wise to have a few cans of beans in your pantry for those inevitable times when you need to make a quick soup, salad, or whatever, but have no time to soak them.

A soaking and boiling time chart appears overleaf, as the legumes vary enormously in their needs. There also follows a list of some of the various kinds you may want to stock. They are all so versatile – you eat them hot, cold, whole, puréed on bread, as a dip ... and, of course, they

HERBS

I consider a selection of fresh and dried herbs essential for any cook, and the vegetarian is no exception. At the minimum you should try to have a regular supply of fresh *parsley*, *mint*, *basil*, *chives*, *cilantro*, *rosemary*, *sage*, *thyme*, and *garlic*. You can either sow the seed yourself or buy small pots from the supermarket or nursery to put on your windowsill; or you can buy cut fresh leaves in packs, or perhaps in bunches. Cut herbs need to be used within a day or two.

For times when you just can't get hold of a fresh herb, you can chop and freeze most varieties; when thawed, they will offer more flavor and aroma than dried herbs. Even so, there will still be times when you do have to fall back on dried varieties.

Keep dried herbs in opaque jars in a cool place, and throw them out if they have been around more than a few months as they will not do your cooking any favors.

SPICES

If you have a good health-food store, buy your spices from there as prices will probably be lower than at the supermarkets, which never seem to sell spices in large enough jars anyway!

Most spices are best bought whole to be ground yourself as you need them. This is quite easily done using a spice mill, coffee grinder, or mortar and pestle. The flavor and aroma of freshly ground spices is far superior to ready ground, long-stored varieties.

The spices worth stocking up with are *coriander seeds*, *cumin*, *dried whole ginger*, *dried chili peppers*, *saffron*, *turmeric*, *cloves*, and *cardamom*. Buy *fresh ginger* and *fresh chili peppers* when you can.

Of course you will also want *black peppercorns,* and it is useful to have a few spice "mixtures" too, such as *Chinese five-spice powder* or *Thai seven-spice*.

CONDIMENTS AND OTHER INGREDIENTS

To make your cooking creative and delicious, here is a list of what I consider essential in the way of bottles, jars, and cans you should keep in stock. You may well add some of your own, but all committed vegetarians should check labels carefully as not all condiments that seem to be vegetarian actually are. For instance, Worcestershire sauce contains anchovies, and Thai curry paste contains shrimp.

Garlic purée: in tubes or jars is a handy standby and sometimes even better in a recipe than chopped fresh garlic.

Tomato paste: important for so many recipes.

Canned tomatoes: when fresh tomatoes are insipid or under-ripe, canned tomatoes are always preferable.

Passata (sieved tomato purée): keep a couple of jars or cans of tomato purée for sauces and casseroles; it is indispensable.

Worcestershire sauce: you can buy anchovy-free sauce at the health-food store.

Black bean sauce and *yellow bean sauce*: these Asian soybean condiments are ideal for quick stir-fries and for marinating tofu.

Plum sauce: another nice stir-fry addition.

Soy sauce: you can buy light or dark; shoyu is the natural and best soy.

Canned or frozen unsweetened coconut milk: brands vary in their taste and their "freshness" feel; try a few until you find one that tastes as good as freshly made coconut milk!

Yeast extract: adds taste and color to stocks, soups, sauces, casseroles.

Sea salt: use freshly ground crystals sparingly in recipes.

Agar-agar: vegetarian alternative to gelatin, available from health-food stores.

Bouillon cubes: most vegetable bouillon cubes aren't terrific – they seem very salty for one thing – but it may be useful to keep some for emergencies. Otherwise, you can use yeast extract or stock concentrate in a jar. You can also buy cartons of chilled vegetable stock, which may be better than stock cubes. These stocks will also freeze.

Canned peppers (pimientos): I keep one can of mixed peppers for use with tomato or zucchini in ratatouilles or stir-fries as a quick side vegetable. I also keep a can of piquillo peppers – delicious Spanish peppers that are costly but make a superb first course, just drizzled with a little olive oil and dusted with black pepper.

Canned or bottled artichoke hearts: keep for first courses, mixed salads, and rice salads, for roasting with other vegetables – in fact they have dozens of delicious uses!

Pickles and chutneys: a jar of good-quality chutney livens up a quick lunch of crusty bread and cheese; a good eggplant or lime relish goes well with all Asian dishes. Your health-food store will have a wide selection.

Water chestnuts: have a can ready to give crunch to vegetable stir-fries.

Bamboo shoots: also good in Chinese stir-fries.

Oils: you will, of course, want some good-quality olive oil for salads and perhaps some mid-quality for cooking. You will also need sunflower oil for a lighter taste in certain recipes. Oriental sesame oil (made from roasted seeds) is the best oil to use for Asian dishes, while walnut oil makes a nice salad dressing. Keep a bottle of corn oil for general-purpose cooking.

Store oils in cool, dark conditions and use fairly quickly – walnut oil, in particular, goes rancid within weeks.

Vinegars: have a stock of three or four vinegars, such as a good red wine and white wine vinegar, plus a cider vinegar and a sherry vinegar. They last for ages and are good for dressings, marinades, and all kinds of dishes.

SWEETENERS

A little sugar isn't going to do you harm, so keep some on hand. Brown sugar isn't really any better than white, so the choice is yours. Fructose (fruit sugar) is indispensable for cooking, as it is twice as sweet as sucrose (sugar) and isn't absorbed into the bloodstream so quickly. Unless you are a strict vegan you will also want some clear honey.

SHORT CUTS TO GOOD FOOD

For the cook in a hurry, there are various ways you can save time in the vegetarian kitchen:

∗ Use canned ready-cooked beans and lentils, rather than soaking and cooking your own.

∗ Invest in a pressure cooker to cut down on time cooking soups, stews, dried beans, and vegetables.

∗ You can buy frozen ready-cooked rice as a standby. It isn't quite as good as freshly cooked rice, but can be pepped up with a few additions.

∗ Think "pasta": keep a good stock of pasta shapes and varieties; all cook within 10–12 minutes and provide delicious, nutritious suppers with …

∗ Sauces! When you aren't so busy, batch-cook some sauces (e.g. tomato, lentil, spinach) and freeze them. You can even stock a couple of ready-made sauces in jars – some Italian pasta sauces are quite good and fresh ones from the refrigerated section at the supermarket are even better. Not all are low in fat, so check the label.

∗ Microwave – I have never managed to achieve brilliant results cooking recipes from scratch in a microwave oven. They are, however, very useful for thawing sauces, soups, fruit purées, and breads, so it is worth investing in a small microwave if you are permanently busy or have a lone vegetarian in the household. With a microwave, baked potatoes can be cooked in a few minutes and topped with a sauce or lowfat cheese.

∗ For cold weather: soups and stir-fries. Many of the soup recipes in this book are quick to make, as are many of the suppers and lunches. When cooking a recipe that will freeze, always make double the quantity to provide you with an instant meal another day.

∗ For hot weather: bread and cheese, or bread and a spread or dip such as those on pages 63–6, are quick and ideal. Add salad for a perfect balanced meal.

∗ Eggs: if you eat eggs, a frittata-style (flat) omelet with vegetables is quick and delicious once or twice a week, as is a soufflé omelet or scrambled eggs with fresh herbs and bread.

NON-VEGETARIAN INGREDIENTS

Non-vegetarian ingredients: cochineal, pepsin, gelatin, glycerine, hydrolyzed proteins, rennet, glycerol, aspic, stearates.

Notes: hydrolyzed vegetable protein is all right. Sometimes lecithin (often added to margarine and chocolate) is produced from other than free-range eggs, so is not always suitable for vegans or lacto-vegetarians.

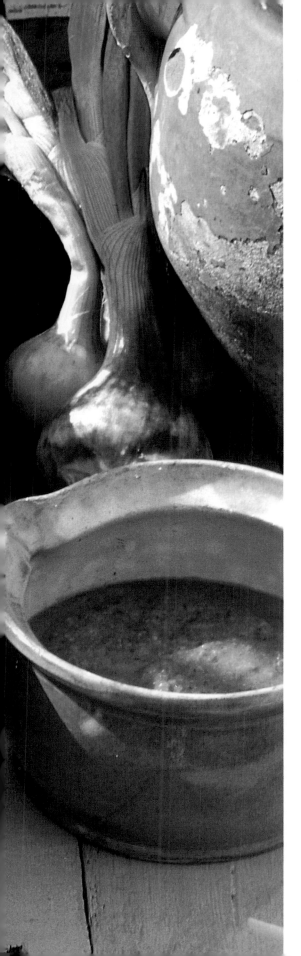

Planning your own diet

Here you will find out how to balance your own daily diet – for good health as well as enjoyment – and put into practice all the ideas you learned in the previous chapters.

At the start of this book we looked at the different elements that make up a healthy, well-balanced vegetarian diet. This chapter will help you translate all that knowledge into enjoyable daily and weekly menus.

I have devised the five plans that appear later in this chapter as examples of some of the many different and delicious ways you can eat to suit yourself, secure in the knowledge that you are eating within World Heath Organization guidelines.

The seven-day plans show how the recipes from the later chapters of the book can be incorporated into a healthy overall diet, which will be high in carbohydrates and fiber, low in fat, and with adequate protein, vitamins, and minerals. If you need to lose weight, turn to the next chapter.

By using one or two of these plans and trying out the different recipes, you will soon get a "feel" for eating a vegetarian diet that is not only pleasurable but also nutritious and well balanced. The plans are all suitable in calorie content for most women to maintain their current weight. Men may need to add extra calories in the form of more bread, potatoes, rice, cereals, and legumes to one or two meals a day, or take extra between-meal snacks of these foods and perhaps some extra fruit.

When you've tried out some of the plans that suit you, you will, of course, want to begin building your own daily and weekly menus. You can be sure of getting a healthy diet if you stick to the following common-sense principles:

★ Build each meal – or at least most of them – around a high-carbohydrate food (such as rice or another grain, pasta, potatoes, beans, bread, and pizza).

★ Add some high-protein, lowfat food to this basic food if necessary. Remember that most of the high-carbohydrate foods (such as legumes and whole grains) are also good sources of protein in themselves. If adding dairy products, add only small amounts.

These first two ingredients of the meal will together almost certainly form your "complete" protein (see pages 10–11).

High-protein foods you may like to add include tofu, egg, cheese, skim milk, and soy milk. Higher in fat are nuts and seeds, which should be added in moderation.

* Now add plenty of lightly cooked fresh vegetables or raw salads.

* Add fruit to most meals. If the "main course" has been fairly low in protein, you can add a lowfat, high-protein dessert, such as cottage cheese or yogurt.

If you keep choosing first a large portion of carbohydrate, and then add a smaller amount of protein foods and plenty of fruit and vegetables, you can't go wrong!

EXAMPLES:

BREAKFAST

1   Choose a high-carbohydrate food, such as a whole-grain cereal.

2   Add high-protein skim milk or soy milk.

3   Add a piece of fresh fruit.

LUNCH

1   Choose a high-carbohydrate food, like bread.

2   Add a high-protein food, e.g. lentil pâté.

3   Add a large mixed salad.

(You could also add some yogurt or a piece of fresh fruit to this meal.)

EVENING

1   Choose a high-carbohydrate food, like rice.

2 and 3   Add a high-protein food and fresh vegetables, e.g. tofu and vegetable stir-fry.

(You could add fresh fruit to this meal.)

OR

Choose one of the ready-balanced recipe dishes that appear in the chapters on Quick Suppers and Lunches (page 70) or Main Courses (page 82). This may be a complete meal in itself or there may be serving suggestions with it – or you could pick one of the meal suggestions from one of the plans (pages 35–9 and 45–9).

If you don't have to worry about your weight at all (some people can eat lots more than others without ever gaining weight), then you can also add one of the healthy desserts from the Sweet Treats chapter (see page 106), or something else of your own. You could instead perhaps even snack on some of the healthy treats in that same chapter between meals.

The only other "rules" to bear in mind are that all fats and oils should be added sparingly to foods. For example, don't coat your hunk of bread with a slab of butter as a matter of habit, or you will be undoing the good that the rest of your healthy diet is doing you! Use fat only when really necessary to add flavor, brown and seal food, or add moisture, as in a dressing.

It is also important not to stick to the same few food items day in and day out – experiment with new foods, new recipes, new fruits and vegetables, and you are bound to get all the nutrients you need for health.

USING THE RECIPES

Many of the main-meal, supper, and lunch recipes in the later chapters are perfectly balanced nutritionally – high in carbohydrate, low in fat, and with adequate protein, vitamins, and minerals. However, the proportions of these constituents do vary, so each recipe incorporates a nutrition information panel to help you build your balanced diet. Here is an explanation of how to use these in working out a healthy daily diet:

* CALORIE counts are self-explanatory. If female, build a diet based on around 2,000 calories a day; if male, on around 2,700 a day.

* TOTAL FAT content is given as "High," "Medium," or "Low." "High" means that the recipe contains over 35% total fat content (of total calorie content of the recipe). In most cases, any recipe included in this book with a high total fat content will be eaten with a lowfat, high-carbohydrate accompaniment (e.g. bread with a high-fat dip.) However, by most standards, none of the recipes in this book is very high in fat – otherwise it wouldn't have been included. "Medium" fat content means the recipe contains between 20% and 35% fat. If the carbohydrate content of a medium-fat meal is high, it will then give you a reasonably well-balanced meal in itself. "Low" means the recipe contains less than 20% fat. If you choose such a dish you could then, perhaps, add another higher-fat dish to the menu without feeling guilty (e.g. a baked casserole or dessert, or some grated cheese).

* SATURATED FAT content is also given. This is because it is the saturated fats in our diet that we should

be making most efforts to cut down – the W.H.O. has given a level of saturated fat of 10% of the total daily calories as ideal. Here, therefore, "high" means the recipe contains over 10% of its total calories as saturated fat; "medium" means it contains from 5% to 10%; and "low" means it contains less than 5%. These saturated fat figures are, of course, not in addition to the total fat figures.

★ CARBOHYDRATE content is given as "High," "Medium," or "Low." "High" means that the recipe contains over 50% of its calories as carbohydrate, "medium" means between 40% and 50%, and "low" means it has less than 40%. You will find that "low-carbohydrate" recipes are almost always to be eaten with high-carbohydrate accompaniments (e.g. bread, rice, or potatoes).

Any high-carbohydrate savory dish will also be high in fiber. Some of the bakes and desserts are not necessarily high in fiber as their carbohydrate content may be in the form of simple sugars or fructose that contain no fiber. However, these recipes are intended to be eaten in small quantities, so there is no need to worry about including them in your diet.

★ PROTEIN content is given as "High," "Medium," or "Low." "High" means the recipe contains over 15% of its calories as protein, "medium" means it contains between 5% and 15%, "low" means it contains under 5%. As normal protein intake averages out at around 10%–15% a day, you could balance a low-protein meal with a high-protein meal at another time of day, or add a high-protein dessert.

★ CHOLESTEROL content is given in milligrams for people who have been advised by their doctor to keep a check on their blood cholesterol levels. For most of us it is more important to watch our fat intake levels and get enough fruit and vegetables.

★ VITAMINS are named when that particular vitamin is found in good quantities in that recipe. The vitamins are listed starting with the one found in greatest quantity and so on. Vitamins other than those listed may be present in the recipe, but not in such significant amounts.

★ MINERALS are listed in the same manner as vitamins.

As I said earlier, if you are eating a wide variety of foods you should automatically get all the vitamins and minerals you need for good health, but if you would like to make sure, these nutritional information panels give you a more thorough check.

Now, if you need to lose some weight or have someone in the family who would like to diet, turn to the next chapter!

THE VEGAN PLAN

*Seven days of tempting meals with no dairy products at all.
About 2,000 calories per day*

Extras per day: 1 cup soy milk, 2 glasses of wine or 200 calories' worth of any item from the Sweet Treats chapter (page 106), and 1 tablespoon vegetable margarine for use on bread and/or as a garnish.

Stuffed Vegetables

DAY ONE
BREAKFAST
2 *Reduced-Fat Scones* with
   pure fruit spread
1 orange

LUNCH
Avocado and Leaf Salad
1 large wholewheat roll
1 large banana

EVENING
Delhi-Style Cauliflower
   (made using soy "yogurt")
Chana Masaledar
1 cup boiled brown rice
chutney of choice
fresh sliced mango, dressed
   with lime juice and served
   with non-dairy cream

DAY TWO
BREAKFAST
Granola with soy milk
   (extra to allowance)
1 apple or peach

LUNCH
Avocado and Tofu Dip with
   crudités
Black Bean Soup with
   3 ounces French bread
ready-made soy "yogurt"
   dessert

EVENING
Guacamole with toasted
   bread sticks
Vegetable Paella
Marinated Strawberries

DAY THREE
BREAKFAST
⅓ cup baked beans on
   2 large slices of
   wholewheat toast
1 orange

LUNCH
3 ounces egg-free pasta of
   choice (dry weight), boiled
   and topped with
Tomato Sauce
⅓ cup nuts and raisins

EVENING
Spicy Stuffed Vegetables
*Baked Banana with Lemon
   and Orange*
1 portion of soy "ice cream"

DAY FOUR
BREAKFAST
Fruit Compote
1 slice of *Banana and
   Walnut Bread*
1 glass of orange juice

LUNCH
1 slice of cold *Cashew Roast*
large mixed salad
4 ounces cooked new
   potatoes or brown rice
*Orange and Watercress
   Salad*

EVENING
Cobbler-Topped Casserole
1 large portion of leafy
   greens, lightly cooked
one 6-ounce baked potato
1 cooking apple, cored and
   filled with dried fruit of
   choice and 2 teaspoons
   brown sugar, then baked

DAY FIVE
BREAKFAST
1 glass of orange juice
2 *Reduced-Fat Scones* with
   Banana Spread

LUNCH
*Brown Rice Salad with
   Mushrooms and Beans*
1 wholewheat roll
1 kiwi fruit or peach

EVENING
Three-Bean Casserole
one 5-ounce sweet potato,
   baked
large mixed salad with *Oil-
   Free Vinegar Dressing*
Baked Peaches with soy "ice
   cream"

DAY SIX
BREAKFAST
Special Recipe Muesli with
   soy milk (extra to
   allowance)
½ portion of *Fruit Compote*

LUNCH
1 glass of orange juice
Lentil Pâté with 3 ounces
   crusty bread
Fruit Coleslaw
1 large banana

EVENING
Italian Artichokes
1 wholewheat roll
3 ounces egg-free pasta,
   boiled, with
Mediterranean Sauce and
   1 tablespoon pine nuts
   sprinkled over

DAY SEVEN
BREAKFAST
2 slices of bread with
   Cashew-Nut Spread
1 orange
½ portion of *Fruit Compote*

LUNCH
*Curried Lentil and Vegetable
   Soup*
2 *Scottish Oatcakes*
4 ounces grapes or plums

EVENING
Marinated Mushrooms
1 slice of rye or wholewheat
   bread
Bombay Supper
1 apple

Plums

FAST AND SIMPLE

In this seven-day plan the accent is on meals that are easy and quick to prepare and cook.
About 2,000 calories per day

Extras per day: **1 cup skim milk, 2 glasses of wine or 200 calories' worth of any item from the Sweet Treats chapter (page 106) or similar, and 1 tablespoon butter or vegetable margarine for use on bread and/or as a garnish.**

Pasta spirals with spinach sauce

DAY ONE
BREAKFAST
2 *Scottish Oatcakes* with *Banana Spread*
1 pear or peach
1 portion of plain lowfat yogurt with 1 teaspoon clear honey

LUNCH
2 slices of wholewheat bread filled with 1 tablespoon peanut butter and salad
1 orange

EVENING
Summer Frittata
large mixed salad
3 ounces French bread
Fruit Coleslaw

DAY TWO
BREAKFAST
2 slices of bread, toasted and topped with *Cashew-Nut Spread*
1 glass of grapefruit or mixed citrus fruit juice
1 portion of plain lowfat yogurt with 1 teaspoon of clear honey

LUNCH
Lentil Pâté with 1 large wholewheat roll
Endive, Orange, and Date Salad
1 large banana

EVENING
3 ounces pasta spirals, boiled, with
Spinach Sauce and 2 tablespoons grated Parmesan cheese
1 apple

DAY THREE
BREAKFAST
Granola with milk (extra to allowance)
1 glass of orange juice
1 slice of wholewheat bread with pure fruit spread

LUNCH
Mushroom Spread on 3 slices of rye crispbread
Leek and Chive Soup
1 peach or pear
1 slice of *Caribbean Cake*

EVENING
Hot Cheese and Olive Platter
1 large crusty roll
1 large banana

DAY FOUR
BREAKFAST
1 large portion of lowfat plain yogurt sprinkled with ½ portion of *Special Recipe Muesli* and 1 piece of fresh fruit of choice, chopped, or 4 ounces soft fruit

LUNCH
small French loaf spread with *Mexican-Style Dip* and filled with crisp lettuce and tomato

EVENING
Tofu Kebabs with Peanut Sauce
½ cup Thai fragrant rice, boiled
Hazelnut Ice Cream

DAY FIVE
BREAKFAST
Wheat Flakes with skim milk (extra to allowance)
1 large slice of bread with pure fruit spread
1 apple

LUNCH
1 large crusty roll filled with *Red Lentil Spread*
Fruit Coleslaw
1 fruit yogurt

EVENING
Chinese Egg and Noodle Stir-Fry
1 portion of lychees with lowfat soft cheese

DAY SIX
BREAKFAST
Special Recipe Muesli with skim milk (extra to allowance)
1 glass of orange juice

LUNCH
¾ cup cooked brown rice mixed with ½ ripe chopped avocado and 1 portion of *Fresh Tomato Salsa*
3 ounces crusty bread

EVENING
Three-Bean Casserole
one 7-ounce baked potato
lightly cooked broccoli or snow peas
Baked Banana with Lemon and Orange

DAY SEVEN
BREAKFAST
Same as Day Three

LUNCH
3 Scottish Oatcakes with 2½ ounces Brie or Camembert or half-fat vegetarian Cheddar cheese
large tomato and onion salad
1 slice of *Caribbean Cake*

EVENING
Fettuccine with Wine and Mushrooms
large mixed leaf salad with *Oil-Free Vinegar Dressing*
selection of fruits with 1 tablespoon whole-milk yogurt or crème fraîche

THE FAMILY PLAN

Robust and interesting meals that all the family will enjoy.
About 2,000 calories per day

Extras per day: 1 cup skim milk (whole milk for children under 5), 2 glasses wine or 200 calories' worth of any item from the Sweet Treats chapter (page 106), and 1 tablespoon butter or vegetable margarine for use on bread and/or as a garnish.

Baked apples with raisins + honey

DAY ONE
BREAKFAST
Granola with skim milk
  (extra to allowance) with
  1 large banana chopped in
1 glass of orange juice
1 apple

LUNCH
*Curried Lentil and Vegetable
  Soup* (for small children
  you can omit most of the
  curry powder)
1 pita bread
1 fruit-flavored low fat
  yogurt

EVENING
*Macaroni, Red Pepper, and
  Broccoli Bake*
1 portion of green leafy
  vegetable, lightly cooked
2 *Peach and Raisin Cookies*

DAY TWO
BREAKFAST
1 glass of orange juice
Fruit Compote
1 portion of plain lowfat
  yogurt

LUNCH
Pistou with 3 ounces rye
  bread
1 peach or pear

EVENING
*Cheese and Onion Bread
  Bake* or *Hereford Hotpot*
green salad
1 baked apple, cored and
  filled with raisins and
  honey
1 portion of lowfat cream
  cheese

DAY THREE
BREAKFAST
2 large tomatoes, sliced and
  broiled on 1 large slice of
  wholewheat toast
1 glass of apple juice
1 large banana

LUNCH
Guacamole with crudités
*Classic Three-Bean Salad
  with Pasta*

EVENING
Eggplant and Lentil Layer
½ cup brown rice, boiled
mixed salad
stewed fruit, such as apricots
  with 2 tablespoons whole-
  milk yogurt

DAY FOUR
BREAKFAST
Special Recipe Muesli with
  skim milk (extra to
  allowance) and
2 pieces of fresh fruit of
  choice, chopped in

LUNCH
Parsley and Potato Soup
Red Lentil Spread on 2 slices
  of wholewheat toast
salad of fresh beansprouts
  mixed with grated beet
  and apple, all tossed in
  Light Vinaigrette

EVENING
*Provençal Crêpes with
  Cheese Sauce*
green leaf salad
fresh fruit salad with
  2 tablespoons of whole-
  milk yogurt

DAY FIVE
BREAKFAST
2 *Pineapple Muffins*
1 orange

LUNCH
10-ounce baked potato with
  Chana Masaledar
large mixed salad

EVENING
Crispy Vegetable Pie
6 ounces new potatoes
1 portion of leafy greens
Summer Pudding
whole-milk yogurt

DAY SIX
BREAKFAST
2 slices of wholewheat
  bread with *Banana Spread*
1 portion of plain lowfat
  yogurt with 1 teaspoon
  clear honey
1 glass of orange juice

LUNCH
1 *Pizza Base* topped with
  Tomato Sauce, sliced
  mushrooms, seeded and
  chopped green and yellow
  sweet peppers, and
  Mozzarella cheese
crisp green salad
1 slice of *Caribbean Cake*

EVENING
Mexican-Style Dip with toast
  fingers
Spicy Stuffed Vegetables
8-ounce baked potato
mixed salad
Fruit Compote with *Granola*
  topping

DAY SEVEN
BREAKFAST
As Day Two

LUNCH
Leek and Chive Soup with
  ½ tablespoon sesame
  seeds or 1 ounce
  vegetarian Cheddar
  cheese grated on top
1 wholewheat roll
1 large banana

EVENING
3 ounces spaghettini, boiled
  and topped with
Lentil Sauce
green salad
Hazelnut Ice Cream

LATE PREGNANCY

In the first few months of pregnancy, you hardly need to eat any extra calories. In the last few months, however, you should add around 300 calories a day extra, and have plenty of iron, calcium, and vitamin C.
About 2,300 calories per day

Extras per day: 2 cups skim milk, ½ cup plain lowfat yogurt (with a little honey if you like), 200 calories' worth of any item from the Sweet Treats chapter (see page 106), and 1 tablespoon butter or vegetable margarine for use on bread and/or as a garnish.

Pea + watercress soup

DAY ONE
BREAKFAST
Special Recipe Muesli with *Fruit Compote* and skim milk (extra to allowance)
1 glass of orange juice

LUNCH
Marinated Mushrooms
Gado Gado
1 large banana
1 portion of cottage cheese

EVENING
Falafel Patties
Fresh Tomato Salsa
1 wholewheat pita bread
large mixed salad
Baked Peach

DAY TWO
BREAKFAST
1 large wholewheat roll spread with yeast extract
1 small bowl of high-bran cereal with skim milk (extra to allowance)
1 orange

LUNCH
Cheese and Walnut Dip as a spread in a French bread roll
Winter Red Salad or tomato and basil salad

EVENING
Polenta and Sweet Peppers
Tomato Sauce
mixed salad with *Light Vinaigrette*
Marinated Strawberries with whole-milk yogurt

DAY THREE
BREAKFAST
As Day One

LUNCH
Avocado and Tofu Dip with crudités and strips of pita bread
Pea and Watercress Soup
1 *Pineapple Muffin*

EVENING
Broccoli and Corn Quiche
7 ounces new potatoes or cooked brown rice
green salad
salad of mixed fresh beansprouts with sliced raw mushrooms and *Oil-Free Vinegar Dressing*
Baked Banana with Lemon and Orange

DAY FOUR
BREAKFAST
2 slices of wholewheat bread
1 large poached egg
1 orange
1 apple

LUNCH
Parsley and Potato Soup
1 small French roll
1 large banana

EVENING
Grilled Vegetables with Bulghur
Apricot Slice

DAY FIVE
BREAKFAST
Same as Day One

LUNCH
Summer Frittata
large slice of wholewheat bread
large mixed salad
1 fruit-flavored lowfat yogurt

EVENING
Mushroom Pilaf
green salad with *Light Vinaigrette*
Lemon and Lime Sorbet

DAY SIX
BREAKFAST
Same as Day Two

LUNCH
large wholewheat roll filled with *Cashew-Nut Spread*
Fruit Coleslaw
1 banana

EVENING
Provençal Crêpes with Cheese Sauce
green salad with *Light Vinaigrette*
Fruit Compote with whole-milk yogurt

DAY SEVEN
BREAKFAST
Same as Day Four

LUNCH
Spanish Chickpeas
1 pita bread
green salad
Apricot Slice

EVENING
Rich Potato Bake
1 portion of lightly cooked broccoli
Hazelnut Ice Cream

Grilled Vegetables

DINNER PARTY MENUS

Meat-eaters and non meat-eaters alike will enjoy these seven different vegetarian dinner party menus. Six of them have their own ethnic theme and one is specially devised for vegans.

With calorie counts as low as these – particularly the Spanish and Italian menus – you need not feel guilty about a glass or two of wine with the meal.

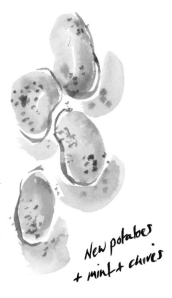

New potatoes + mint + chives

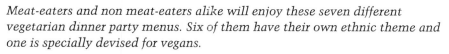

Mixed pepper Croustades

MENU ONE
ASIAN STYLE

About 990 calories

Hot and Sour Soup

* * * * *

Thai-Style Mixed Vegetables

Thai fragrant rice
Bakmie Goreng

* * * * *

Lemon and Lime Sorbet
fresh lychees

MENU TWO
INDIAN-STYLE

About 1,050 calories

Chana Masaledar with naan
  bread

* * * * *

Bombay Supper
Delhi-Style Cauliflower
plain yogurt with chopped
  cucumber and chopped
  fresh cilantro
selection of chutneys

* * * * *

fresh mangoes and
  kumquats

MENU THREE
BRITISH-STYLE

About 950 calories

Pea and Watercress Soup

* * * * *

Crispy Vegetable Pie
new potatoes with chopped
  mint and chives
baby corn
snow peas

* * * * *

Summer Pudding with half-
  and-half cream

MENU FOUR
FRENCH-STYLE

About 1,000 calories

*Marinated Eggplant and
  Tomato*

* * * * *

Cheese and Tomato Roulade
*Hot Baby Vegetables with
  Red Pesto*
mixed leaf salad with *Oil-
  Free Vinegar Dressing*

* * * * *

meringue with *Marinated
  Strawberries* and crème
  fraîche

MENU FIVE
SPANISH-STYLE

About 900 calories

Mixed Pepper Croustades

* * * * *

Vegetable Paella
mixed leaf salad with *Light
  Vinaigrette*

* * * * *

fresh fruit platter with a
  selection of vegetarian
  cheeses

MENU SIX
ITALIAN-STYLE

About 750 calories

Italian Artichokes

* * * * *

*Fettuccine with Wine and
  Mushrooms*
mixed salad

* * * * *

Baked Peaches with Italian
  ice cream

MENU SEVEN
VEGAN

About 720 calories

Avocado and Tofu Dip with
  crudités

* * * * *

Carrot and Tomato Soup

* * * * *

*Grilled Vegetables with
  Bulghur*
*Orange and Watercress
  Salad*

* * * * *

*Baked Bananas with Lemon
  and Orange*

Menu planning for weight loss

The vegetarian style of eating is very suitable for helping you to shed weight if you so wish. This chapter contains diet plans and advice to make the process both pleasant and easy.

A recent British Government Survey (*Health Survey for England, 1991*) showed that, despite the barrage of healthy eating advice that has been available for the past decade or more, the number of overweight and obese (very overweight) people in Great Britain has risen since 1986.

On average, vegetarians are less likely than the rest of the population to suffer from obesity. So making the change from a carnivorous to a vegetarian diet should – if you tend to be over-weight – help you in your dieting campaign.

A few vegetarians, however, do put on weight – some, per-haps, because they don't take enough exercise; but others, I am sure, because they still eat a great deal of fat in the form of dairy products, nuts, and sweets and cakes.

The diet plans that follow show five different ways to combine the recipes in this book with other foods to allow you – or your partner or family – to lose weight successfully.

Look through the plans and, if you happen to be a vegetarian with a weight problem, you will see that there is no need to cut out all the foods you enjoy in order to lose weight. You can still have some dairy products, cheese, desserts … the secret is to limit the overall fat and calorie content of your diet without going on a crash diet, so that you lose weight gradually.

A well-balanced vegetarian diet is ideally suited to help you lose weight without feeling deprived or wanting to give up for two main reasons:

1   It is (or should be) high in complex carbohydrates like bread, grains, and legumes (see the first chapter for more information) – the very foods that, in all tests so far conducted, have been shown to help dieters lose weight painlessly. This is because they actually appear to speed up your metabolic rate, helping you to burn

calories more quickly than if, say, you ate a low-calorie diet consisting mostly of fat. The complex carbohydrates are also very filling, so you don't feel hungry after eating your low-calorie meal. Thirdly, they keep you feeling full longer so you don't get nagging between-meal hunger pangs and cravings.

2 It is (or should be) high in fresh fruits and vegetables, which will automatically add variety and color and yet more f lling power for a few extra calories. Their vitamins and minerals will also keep you healthy while you diet.

So, if you can just control your fat intake (with the help of my recipes in the chapters that follow) you have the perfect recipe for a successful diet!

Pick a plan that suits you and follow it for a week or two, and you will see how pleasant dieting can be. (See overleaf also for a list of foods that you can enjoy at any time on your diet in addition to all the foods in the plans.)

Then, perhaps, when you have lost a few pounds you will want to devise some diet plans of your own for more variety. In that case, these tips will help you:

* First check out the height/weight chart on page 128 and see approximately how much weight you would like to lose (don't aim too low).

* Remember that women should diet on around 1,200 calories a day; men and teenagers on around 1,500.

* Split your daily calories over several meals or snacks, rather than having just, say, one big meal a day. This will stop you from feeling hungry.

* All the recipes in this book are calorie-counted, so you can easily incorporate them into your own diet. The calorie counts of some of the more basic foods are given overleaf so that you can add them to the recipes or devise your own breakfasts, snacks, etc.

* Make sure you have read the first chapter so that you understand the basics of getting a healthy diet – all the advice there applies just as much to you on a weight-loss diet. You keep the same balance – high carbohydrates, low fat, and adequate protein – even though you are reducing the total calorie content of your diet.

* Plan at least several days' meals in advance.

* Give yourself a daily skim or soy milk allowance and daily lowfat spread allowance – and stick to it.

* It may help you plan your diet if you use a notebook to record what you intend to eat each day with its approximate calorie content.

Soups, appetizers, and snacks

Soups and appetizers really are the most versatile of vegetarian dishes – and all the more useful because most are so simple to cook!

Don't think of soups as just winter dishes – at any time of year they can inject variety, taste, nutrition, and filling power into a vegetarian diet. They can perform any role, supporting as a light first course or starring as a substantial lunch or supper, hot or cold, quick and easy, or more elaborate and impressive.

I have selected a cross section of soups for all occasions and all tastes – but each is a particular favorite. When you have tried them you will realize that soup-making isn't difficult and you can perhaps invent some variations of your own.

A good stock is essential in most soups. Almost any combination of vegetables – with legumes for a main-meal soup – can be simmered in the stock, and then puréed or left in chunks. Experiment with herbs and spices for extra flavor. For a healthy soup you don't need to sauté the vegetables in oil beforehand, as recipes often suggest. Neither is there any need to garnish or thicken with cream – plain yogurt will do very well.

The appetizers I have selected can also be used as light lunches if you are watching your weight. A balanced selection of them could also form the basis of a good buffet or a mezze-type first course for a dinner party.

For other ideas, any of the dips on pages 64–5 will make an informal appetizer with toast or crudités. Served in half portions, the main-course salads beginning on page 96 will make good appetizers, as can many other dishes such as, say, the Polenta and Sweet Peppers on page 74.

Don't forget even simpler appetizer ideas, like large stuffed black olives, slices of ripe melon, hummus, or cucumber and yogurt dip with crudités, etc. Remember also to balance the meal: for nutrition and appeal, choose a low-calorie, lowfat appetizer if you have a higher-calorie, higher-fat main course, and vice versa.

Hot and Sour Soup (page 52); Italian Artichokes (page 57)   51

CARROT AND TOMATO SOUP

I find most carrot soups too sweet and bland for my taste, but this has a nice tart bite to it.

Calories per serving: 86
Saturated fat: High
Total fat: High
Protein: Medium
Carbohydrate: Medium
Cholesterol: 3.5 mg
Vitamins: A, C, E
Minerals: Potassium

1 tbsp sunflower oil
1½ cups chopped carrots
1 garlic clove, chopped
1 medium onion, finely chopped
1¼ cups peeled and chopped
   tomatoes
1 tsp ground cumin
2 cups *Vegetable Stock*
   (see page 122)
bouquet garni
bay leaf
1 tbsp dry sherry
salt (optional)
¼ cup light cream

Heat the oil in a heavy saucepan, add the carrots, garlic, and onion, and simmer over low heat for 10 minutes.

Add the tomatoes and cumin, cover, and simmer 2 minutes. Add the stock and herbs and simmer 15 minutes more.

Remove the herbs and purée the soup in a blender. Return to the pan, stir in the sherry, and reheat. Taste and add a little salt if desired.

Swirl in the cream before serving.

Note: this soup does benefit from the bit of cream, but if you want to save a little fat and about 12 calories per serving, simply leave the cream out and garnish with chopped parsley.

GREEN PEA AND WATERCRESS SOUP

This soup is just as good served cold as hot. For a change, try shredding some lettuce and adding it to the soup while it reheats.

Calories per serving: 93
Saturated fat: Low
Total fat: Medium
Protein: High
Carbohydrate: High
Cholesterol: None
Vitamins: C, A, E, B group
Minerals: Potassium, Iron,
   Calcium

1 tbsp lowfat spread
1 medium onion, chopped
3⅓ cups *Vegetable Stock*
   (see page 122)
2¼ cups tender frozen peas
1 large bunch of watercress, trimmed,
   washed, and chopped
salt and black pepper
2 tbsp chopped fresh mint

Melt the lowfat spread in a heavy saucepan and sauté the onion until soft.

Add the stock, peas, and watercress. Bring to a boil, then simmer 10 minutes.

Season to taste and purée the soup in a blender. Return to the pan, add the mint, and heat through to serve.

Note: you can add a dash of light cream or plain yogurt to each bowl before serving, which would add only a very few extra calories.

OPPOSITE: **Carrot and Tomato Soup; Green Pea and Watercress Soup**

MARINATED MUSHROOMS WITH CILANTRO

Serve fresh crusty French bread to mop up the delicious sauce.

Calories per serving: 50
Saturated fat: Medium
Total fat: High
Protein: Medium
Carbohydrate: Low
Cholesterol: None
Vitamins: C, A, E
Minerals: Potassium

12 ounces button mushrooms
3 tbsp white wine vinegar
1 tbsp lemon juice
1 tbsp olive oil
1 garlic clove, chopped
1 small bay leaf
pinch of brown sugar
1 tsp ground coriander
½ cup tomato purée
salt and black pepper
2 tbsp chopped fresh parsley or
    cilantro

Brush the mushrooms clean, if necessary, and place them in a bowl.

Put all the remaining ingredients except the chopped fresh herbs in a small pan, season well, and bring to a boil, stirring. Simmer 2 minutes.

Pour this over the mushrooms and let marinate several hours, or overnight if possible.

Serve cold or reheated, with the chopped herbs sprinkled over.

MARINATED EGGPLANT AND TOMATO

Nothing could be simpler than this appetizer, which could also be served as a side vegetable.

Calories per serving: 90
Saturated fat: Medium
Total fat: High
Protein: Medium
Carbohydrate: Low
Cholesterol: None
Vitamins: A, C, E
Minerals: Potassium

3 tbsp balsamic vinegar
2 tbsp olive oil
2 garlic cloves, crushed
black pepper
2 small eggplants
2 beef tomatoes
2 tbsp chopped fresh basil

Preheat the broiler.

Make a dressing by mixing together the vinegar, olive oil, garlic, and pepper. Trim the eggplants, cut into rounds about ½-inch thick, and brush with half the dressing.

Broil until golden on both sides, about 3 minutes per side, turning once.

Slice the tomatoes horizontally into rounds and arrange on a serving dish (or individual dishes) with the cooked eggplant slices. Pour the remaining dressing over and let marinate an hour or two.

Just before serving, sprinkle with basil.

CROSTINI

These traditional little Italian snacks also make ideal buffet fare, or a light lunch in themselves if you're watching the calories.

Calories per serving: 126
Saturated fat: Medium
Total fat: Medium
Protein: Medium
Carbohydrate: Medium
Cholesterol: 3.5 mg
Vitamins: A, C, E, Folic acid
Minerals: Potassium, Calcium

1 medium eggplant
1 tbsp olive oil
1 medium yellow onion, finely
    chopped
1 large garlic clove, crushed
1½ cups sliced mushrooms
4 pitted green olives, chopped
1 cup canned crushed tomatoes,
    drained
¼ cup diced Italian buffalo Mozzarella
1 tsp chopped fresh or dried basil
salt and black pepper
4 medium-thick slices of Italian bread

Preheat the oven to 375°F. Bake the eggplant in the oven until tender, about 45 minutes. Let cool slightly, then cut in half and scoop out the flesh.

Meanwhile, heat the oil in a nonstick frying pan and sauté the onion and garlic until soft, stirring frequently. When they are just turning golden, add the mushrooms and cook 3 minutes, stirring.

Add the eggplant to the pan with the olives, tomatoes, basil, cheese, and seasoning. Stir and simmer 5 minutes.

Toast the bread and top with the mixture. Cut into fingers or triangles to serve.

OPPOSITE: Marinated Mushrooms with Cilantro; Marinated Eggplant and Tomato

MIXED PEPPER CROUSTADES

You need four large muffin cups or individual tart pans for this recipe.

Calories per serving: 128
Saturated fat: Low
Total fat: High
Protein: Medium
Carbohydrate: High
Cholesterol: None
Vitamins: A, C, E
Minerals: Potassium, Iron

1 tbsp olive oil, plus more for brushing
4 thin slices of bread, cut into
    3½-inch rounds
1 small onion, sliced
10 ounces mixed sweet peppers
    (including at least one red), seeded
    and chopped into diamonds
1 garlic clove, chopped
1 cup canned crushed tomatoes,
    drained
1 tsp chopped fresh or dried basil
salt and black pepper
black olives, halved, for garnish

Preheat the oven to 350°F.

Brush the muffin cups or pans lightly with olive oil and press the bread slices in to line them. Brush the bread lightly with oil and bake them until pale golden, about 10 minutes.

Meanwhile, heat the tablespoon of oil in a nonstick frying pan and sauté the onion and peppers, stirring frequently, until they are very soft and golden at the edges, about 20 minutes. Add the garlic and stir a minute. Add the tomatoes, herbs, and seasoning and stir 3 minutes.

Spoon the pepper mixture into the croustades and serve, garnished with olives.

LENTIL PATE

This tasty and satisfying pâté is simple to make and can be adapted for use as a spread or a dip by adding more stock.

Calories per serving: 48
Saturated fat: Low
Total fat: Low
Protein: High
Carbohydrate: High
Cholesterol: None
Vitamins: B group
Minerals: Iron, Magnesium,
    Potassium, Zinc

1 cup *Vegetable Stock*
    (see page 122)
¼ cup Puy or other small lentils
2 scallions, minced
1 tbsp chopped fresh sage
salt and black pepper
more sage leaves, for garnish

Put the stock in a saucepan and add the lentils. Bring to a simmer and cook the lentils until tender, about 30 minutes.

In a blender, purée the cooked lentils and stock together with the scallions and chopped sage. Season to taste.

Spoon into 4 small containers and garnish with sage leaves.

PIQUILLO CREAMS

These are delicious served with crusty bread or toast.

Calories per serving: 58
Saturated fat: Medium
Total fat: Medium
Protein: Medium
Carbohydrate: High
Cholesterol: 5 mg
Vitamins: A, C, E
Minerals: Calcium

6 canned piquillos (Spanish red
    medium-hot peppers), drained and
    chopped
½ cup small-curd cottage cheese
¼ cup lowfat cream cheese
1 tsp garlic paste
pinch of chili powder (optional)
little black pepper
2 tsp balsamic vinegar
2 tbsp very hot water
1 packet (or 1 heaping tsp) of agar-agar
watercress, for garnish

Purée the peppers, cheeses, garlic paste, chili powder if using, black pepper, and vinegar in a blender.

Put the hot water in a small heatproof bowl. Sprinkle the agar-agar into it and stir until dissolved. Add this to the pepper mixture and stir thoroughly.

Divide the mixture among 4 ramekins and chill until set.

Serve in the dishes or unmolded onto plates, garnished with watercress.

Dips, spreads, and sauces

These easy-to-make dips, spreads, and sauces are an indispensable part of the healthy vegetarian diet because they are perfect for snacks and quick meals.

I've combined dips, spreads, and sauces because many are versatile enough to be interchangeable. By my definition a "spread" should be eaten cold and be thin enough to spread easily, but thick enough to stay put when sandwiched. A "dip" is normally eaten cold, is thinner, and is served in a container in which you dip crudités, etc. A "sauce" may be hot or cold and will pour.

I have chosen to categorize the recipes that follow as dips or spreads or sauces, but many can be slightly adapted to turn one into something else! A dip can often be thickened, either by reducing the quantity of liquid in it or by adding bread crumbs, to make a spread. You can also thicken a savory spread (e.g. the Mushroom Spread on page 66) with bread crumbs and turn it into a pâté. The spreads can usually be thinned down with stock, milk, or water to make a dip. The dips may be thinned in the same ways to make sauces. The cooked sauces can be reduced to a dip by simmering them gently until thickened.

Suggestions for using the dips and spreads in your diet appear in the plans on pages 35–9 and 45–9. Most of the sauces are used within other recipes, but here are some more guidelines on using them. The Tomato Sauce you will use frequently to top pasta or pizza, to add moisture and flavor to baked dishes, or as the basis of soups and casseroles. Make plenty and freeze it. You can vary the basic recipe with added herbs, chili, mushrooms, or garlic. The Mediterranean and Lentil Sauces are ideal for pasta, rice, or baked potatoes, or with eggs. The Cheese Sauce is used in Mornays, lasagnas, moussakas, and baked dishes and with eggs, spinach, and grains. The Sweet-and-Sour is a good sauce to add to all stir-fries, and the Fresh Tomato Salsa is perfect with loaves and patties, as a dipping sauce, or with all Mexican dishes.

Top: Tomato Sauce (page 69); bottom: Sweet-and-Sour Sauce (page 66) served on Crêpes (page 121) filled with asparagus

AVOCADO AND TOFU DIP

Calories per serving: 110
Saturated fat: Medium
Total fat: High
Protein: Medium
Carbohydrate: Low
Cholesterol: None
Vitamins: E, C, Folic acid
Minerals: Potassium,
  Magnesium, Calcium, Iron

1 large ripe avocado
2 tsp lemon juice
4½ ounces silken tofu
2 tsp chopped scallions
1 tsp Tabasco sauce
salt

Peel, seed, and chop the avocado, and toss it with the lemon juice in a blender container. Add the rest of the ingredients, with salt to taste, and blend until smooth.
Note: this makes a good topping for baked potatoes, as well as being a fine dip or spread for crackers.

CHEESE AND WALNUT DIP

Like most nuts, walnuts are high in fat – so the secret is to use them in moderation for added taste and crunch. They are also a good source of minerals.

Calories per serving: 117
Saturated fat: High
Total fat: High
Protein: High
Carbohydrate: Low
Cholesterol: 6 mg
Vitamins A, C, Folic acid
Minerals: Calcium, Iron,
  Magnesium

¾ cup lowfat cottage cheese
1 heaped tbsp grated vegetarian
  Parmesan cheese
1 tbsp olive oil
salt and black pepper
3 tbsp skim milk
2 tbsp chopped scallions
1 tbsp chopped fresh parsley
¼ cup chopped walnuts

Blend the cheeses, oil, and seasoning. Add just enough skim milk to make a soft consistency.
  Add the scallions, parsley, and walnuts and stir well.

MEXICAN-STYLE DIP

Good with corn chips and crispbread or on hot toast, garnished with chopped cucumber.

Calories per serving: 105
Saturated fat: Medium
Total fat: High
Protein: High
Carbohydrate: Medium
Cholesterol: 1 mg
Vitamins: C, E, B group
Minerals: Calcium, Potassium,
  Magnesium, Iron

1 tbsp olive oil
15-ounce can red kidney beans,
  drained (reserving liquid),
  or 1⅔ cups cooked red kidney beans
  plus some of the cooking water
1 small green sweet pepper, seeded
  and chopped
salt
about 1 tsp chili powder
1 tbsp grated pecorino cheese
thick rounds of cucumber, for serving
  (optional)

Heat the oil in a heavy saucepan and add all the ingredients except the cheese, together with chili powder to taste.
  Cook over medium heat for 15 minutes, adding a little reserved bean liquid as necessary to give a medium-textured dip. Taste and add more chili powder if desired.
  Serve hot or cold on rounds of cucumber, if using, topped with the cheese.

GUACAMOLE

Calories per serving: 116
Saturated fat: Low
Total fat: High
Protein: Medium
Carbohydrate: Low
Cholesterol: None
Vitamins: E, C, A
Minerals: Potassium, Iron

1 large ripe avocado
1 tbsp fresh lime juice
1 medium tomato, peeled and
    chopped
1 small garlic clove, minced
2 scallions, chopped
pinch of chili powder
salt and black pepper

Peel and seed the avocado quickly and chop the flesh into a bowl. Quickly mix with the lime juice. Mash together with the rest of the ingredients and season to taste.

Serve with tortilla or corn chips.

Note: the mixture can also be used to stuff tomatoes. Bake 10 minutes in a 375°F oven or microwave on HIGH for 1 minute each tomato.

ABOVE: Guacamole

RED LENTIL SPREAD

Calories per serving: 133
Saturated fat: Low
Total fat: Medium
Protein: High
Carbohydrate: Medium
Cholesterol: None
Vitamins: B group
Minerals: Iron, Potassium,
   Magnesium, Zinc

½ cup red lentils
2 tsp polyunsaturated margarine
1 tbsp olive oil
1 tbsp tomato paste
little lemon juice
salt and pepper

Simmer the lentils in 7 fl oz water until very soft, about 45 minutes.

Mash them together with any remaining water in the pan and the rest of the ingredients, adding lemon juice and seasoning to taste.

CASHEW-NUT SPREAD

Calories per serving: 130
Saturated fat: Medium
Total fat: High
Protein: Medium
Carbohydrate: Low
Cholesterol: None
Vitamins: Folic acid, C
Minerals: Calcium, Iron,
   Potassium

2 tsp olive oil
1 small onion, finely chopped
1 small garlic clove, crushed
¾ cup ground toasted cashew nuts
4½ ounces silken tofu
1 tbsp chopped fresh parsley
salt

Heat the oil in a small heavy frying pan and sauté the onion until soft, adding the garlic for the last minute or so.

Add the onion and garlic to the nuts in a mixing bowl. Add all the remaining ingredients with 3 tablespoons of water and mix together well. Add salt to taste.

MUSHROOM SPREAD

Calories per serving: 65
Saturated fat: High
Total fat: High
Protein: Medium
Carbohydrate: Low
Cholesterol: None
Vitamins: C, B group
Minerals: Calcium

1 tbsp olive oil
1 small onion, finely chopped
2½ cups sliced tasty mushrooms
1 small garlic clove, crushed
⅔ cup fresh brown bread crumbs
¼ cup nonfat cream cheese
2 tsp soy sauce
1 tsp lemon juice
pinch of freshly grated nutmeg
pinch of paprika

Heat the oil in a heavy saucepan and sauté the onion until soft. Add the mushrooms and garlic and sauté a few minutes longer, stirring constantly.

Transfer to a blender, add all the remaining ingredients, and blend until smooth.

SWEET-AND-SOUR SAUCE

This is a good stand-by to add to stir-fries.

Calories per serving: 26
Saturated fat: None
Total fat: Low
Protein: Medium
Carbohydrate: High
Cholesterol: None
Vitamins: C
Minerals: Trace

2 tbsp dark soy sauce
about ½ tsp chili sauce
2 tbsp tomato paste
2 tbsp red wine vinegar
about 2 tsp sugar
1 heaped tsp cornstarch
⅔ cup *Vegetable Stock*
   (see page 122) or water

Put all the ingredients in a small saucepan. Cook over medium heat, stirring all the time, until the sauce thickens. Simmer a few minutes.

Adjust the flavor with a little more chili sauce to get the desired degree of hotness, and a little more sugar or vinegar to get the right sweet-and-sour balance for your taste.

FRESH TOMATO SALSA

The refreshing taste of this sauce goes well with many dishes, such as polenta and nut loaves, and it makes a good topping for crêpes, omelets, or tacos.

Calories per serving: 25
Saturated fat: Low
Total fat: Low
Protein: High
Carbohydrate: High
Cholesterol: None
Vitamins: A, C
Minerals: Potassium

2 tomatoes, peeled and chopped
1 red sweet pepper, seeded and chopped
1 fresh chili pepper, seeded and chopped
salt and black pepper

Put all the ingredients in a blender and blend until you have a sauce that still has some texture to it – i.e. don't over-blend.
Notes: you can add extra flavorings to this sauce to suit your taste: e.g. a small amount of fresh garlic, a dash of wine vinegar for more piquancy, or balsamic vinegar for more depth. Mixed with beans (e.g. kidney beans) and served with a cooked grain, such as bulghur or rice, this salsa makes a meal in itself.

CHEESE SAUCE

This cheese sauce is a lot lower in fat than the usual cheese sauces.

Calories per serving: 110
Saturated fat: High
Total fat: High
Protein: High
Carbohydrate: Low
Cholesterol: 6 mg
Vitamins: B group, A, D
Minerals: Calcium

2 tbsp lowfat spread
3 tbsp plain white flour
1½ cups skim milk
⅔ cup grated lowfat vegetarian Cheddar cheese
1 tsp English mustard powder (optional)
salt and pepper

Melt the lowfat spread in a small nonstick saucepan and add the flour off the heat, stirring well. Return to the heat and cook a minute, stirring, over medium heat.

Remove from the heat and add a little milk, stirring to form a thick sauce. Put back on the heat and gradually add the remaining milk, stirring constantly, until you have a smooth white sauce.

Add the cheese and mustard, if using, and stir until the cheese melts. Taste and adjust the seasoning, if necessary.

MEDITERRANEAN SAUCE

One of my very favorite sauces, this is good for pasta and crêpes. It also makes a good pizza topping.

Calories per serving: 80
Saturated fat: Medium
Total fat: High
Protein: Medium
Carbohydrate: High
Cholesterol: None
Vitamins: A, C, E, Folic acid
Minerals: Potassium

1 medium eggplant
1 tbsp olive oil
1½ large onions, thinly sliced and then chopped
2 garlic cloves, crushed
½ cup tomato purée
16-ounce can crushed tomatoes (with liquid)
8 pitted black olives, chopped
2 tsp chopped fresh basil
salt and black pepper

Trim the eggplant and cut it into *small* cubes. Put in a colander, sprinkle with salt, and let drain 30 minutes. Rinse and pat dry.

Heat the olive oil in a nonstick frying pan and sauté the onions until soft, adding the garlic for the last minute.

Add the eggplant cubes, cover, and simmer very gently for 20 minutes, adding a little tomato purée if it looks very dry at any time.

Add the tomatoes, olives, basil, remaining purée, and seasoning. Simmer, uncovered, for 15 minutes, stirring occasionally. Add extra water at any time as necessary. The sauce should be thick but not too dry.

SPINACH SAUCE

Calories per serving: 53
Saturated fat: Low
Total fat: Low
Protein: High
Carbohydrate: Low
Cholesterol: None
Vitamins: A, C, E, Folic acid
Minerals: Calcium, Iron,
   Potassium

1 pound fresh spinach, washed
1 garlic clove, minced
pinch of ground ginger
⅔ cup lowfat plain yogurt
salt

Put the spinach in a saucepan and heat until it wilts.

Drain and purée in a blender with the rest of ingredients.

Taste and adjust the seasoning, if necessary, before serving with poached eggs or pasta.

TOMATO SAUCE

This is a reduced-fat version of the classic tomato sauce. See note for some variations.

Calories per serving: 60
Saturated fat: Medium
Total fat: High
Protein: Medium
Carbohydrate: Low
Cholesterol: None
Vitamins: A, C
Minerals: Iron, Potassium

1 tbsp olive oil
1 medium onion, minced
1 big garlic clove, chopped
1 pound ripe tomatoes, peeled and
   chopped, *or* 16-ounce can crushed
   tomatoes (with liquid)
2 tsp chopped fresh parsley
1 tbsp tomato paste
1 tsp brown sugar
2 tsp lemon juice
1 bay leaf
2 tsp chopped fresh basil
tomato juice as required
salt and black pepper

Heat the oil in a heavy nonstick pan and sauté the onion gently until very soft, adding the garlic toward the end of this time.

Add the rest of the ingredients, except the basil and tomato juice. Simmer 30 minutes, uncovered. Remove the bay and add the basil.

If the sauce is too thick for your needs, thin it down with a little tomato juice or purée. Taste and adjust the seasoning, if necessary. *Note:* instead of the basil you can flavor this sauce with many other herbs, such as oregano or tarragon; or try adding some fresh green chili peppers or half a can of sliced pimientos at the beginning of simmering time.

LENTIL SAUCE

Calories per serving: 204
Saturated fat: Low
Total fat: Low
Protein: High
Carbohydrate: High
Cholesterol: None
Vitamins: B group, C, A
Minerals: Iron, Potassium,
   Magnesium, Zinc

1 cup red lentils
2 cups *Vegetable Stock*
   (see page 122) or water
2 tsp olive oil
1 medium onion, finely chopped
1 garlic clove, chopped
16-ounce can crushed tomatoes (with
   liquid)
2 tbsp red wine
1 tbsp lemon juice
1 tsp five-spice powder

Simmer the lentils in the stock or water until they are very soft, about 45 minutes.

Meanwhile, heat the oil in a medium heavy nonstick saucepan and stir-fry the onion for a few minutes until soft, adding a dash of water if it gets too dry.

Add the garlic and stir that for a minute. Add the rest of the ingredients, including the lentil mixture. Simmer 15 minutes.

Purée in a blender, or leave unblended for a coarser sauce. Ideal over pasta.

OPPOSITE: Spinach Sauce on pasta

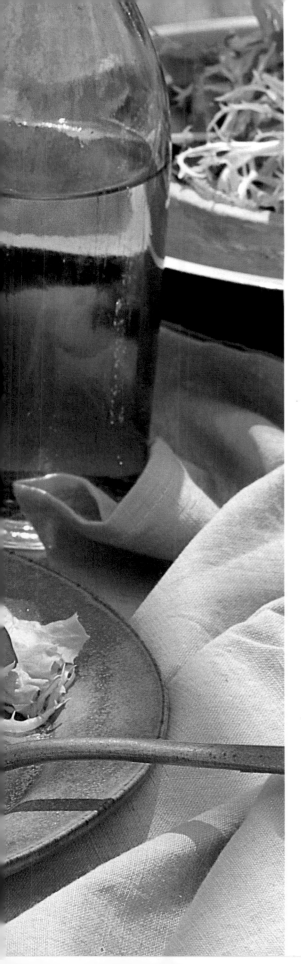

Quick suppers and lunches

When time is short, or if you are eating alone, you'll want something that takes little time to prepare and cook. Here are some of my favorites.

What is the difference between a lunch or supper and a "main meal?" I suppose a main meal consists of more than one dish – or perhaps just one dish consisting of several component parts. It is also, perhaps, a more formal affair. So the recipes in this chapter are all quick, informal, and easy – usually cooked, and sometimes served, in one dish. You'll find more simple, healthy ideas for busy days and hungry people in the plans on pages 35–9 and 45–9.

Cold lunch or supper can be as nutritious as a hot dish. Try a large hunk of rye bread with lowfat cheese and tomatoes or apples. Or, *pan bagna* – a loaf of French bread filled with salad, olives, and hard-boiled egg and drizzled with Light Vinaigrette.

If you have a microwave, potatoes can be baked in minutes and topped with lowfat cottage cheese mixed with mustard or cooked beans in a ready-made chili sauce.

Stir-fries can take a lot of preparation (all that chopping and slicing!), but if you pick baby vegetables, little or no preparation is necessary. Mix in some instant soaked noodles or ready-cooked rice and chopped nuts for a quick treat.

Noodles are also a good – almost instant – base for sauces, as is pasta. If you have a freezer, you can cook up a batch of sauces from the previous chapter and freeze them ready to reheat. Pasta can also be topped even more simply, with garlic or black olives and olive oil, or grated Parmesan and chopped herbs.

Crêpes always make a delicious quick supper, and can be batch-cooked and frozen. Lowfat versions of cheese such as Feta or Mozzarella can be arranged with slices of tomato and herbs and melted in the microwave for a quick lunch. If you eat eggs, it is easy to make an herb omelet and serve it with bread and salad.

Remember that fast cooking retains more of the food's nutrients, so it is doing you good as well as tasting delicious.

Summer Frittata (page 77) and green salad
71

POLENTA AND SWEET PEPPERS

The broiled polenta here is also nice with the **Mediterranean Sauce** *on page 67 instead of the pepper mix.*

Calories per serving: 205
Saturated fat: High
Total fat: High
Protein: Medium
Carbohydrate: Low
Cholesterol: 6.5 mg
Vitamins: A, B group, D
Minerals: Potassium, Iron,
   Calcium

¾ cup polenta or coarse cornmeal
2 tsp chopped fresh basil
⅓ cup grated reduced-fat Cheddar
   cheese
1 tbsp lowfat spread
2 tbsp olive oil
12 ounces mixed sweet peppers,
   seeded and sliced
1 small garlic clove, chopped
3 tbsp dry white wine
2 ounces (½ cup) fresh spinach leaves
2 tsp balsamic vinegar
1 tsp fresh thyme leaves
salt and black pepper

Make the polenta well ahead. Bring 2 cups lightly salted water to a boil and sprinkle in the polenta. Reduce the heat and cook 20 minutes, stirring from time to time, until the polenta comes away from the sides of the pan.

Stir in the basil, cheese, and lowfat spread, then transfer the mixture to a baking pan brushed with ½ tablespoon of olive oil. Let cool and set.

When the polenta is quite solid, heat 1 tablespoon of olive oil in a frying pan and stir-fry the peppers and garlic until soft, about 15 minutes.

Add the wine and bring to a boil. Add the spinach, vinegar, thyme, and seasoning and remove from the heat. Keep hot.

Cut the cooled solidified polenta into about 32 pieces. Brush these with the remaining olive oil and broil 5 minutes. Turn them over and broil until golden. Serve the polenta with the sweet peppers.

HOT CHEESE AND OLIVE PLATTER

This is the quickest supper you could organize. It's a bit higher in fat than is ideal, but it has much less saturated fat and total fat than a typical "cheese and crackers" supper.

Calories per serving: 350
Saturated fat: High
Total fat: High
Protein: High
Carbohydrate: Low
Cholesterol: 50 mg
Vitamins: A, B group, E
Minerals: Calcium, Iron

1 tbsp olive oil
8 ounces Haloumi cheese, cubed
8 pitted black olives
2 sun-dried tomatoes in oil, drained
   and chopped
juice of ½ lemon, for serving
8 ounces French bread, cut into
   4 chunks, for serving

Heat the olive oil in a frying pan over low to medium heat and fry the cheese, olives, and sun-dried tomatoes for a few minutes, turning occasionally.

Sprinkle with lemon juice and serve with hot French bread.

OPPOSITE: Polenta and Sweet Peppers; Hot Cheese and Olive Platter

THREE-BEAN CASSEROLE

You can vary the types of beans used according to what you have in the cupboard.

Calories per serving: 290
Saturated fat: Low
Total fat: Low
Protein: Low
Carbohydrate: High
Cholesterol: None
Vitamins: B group, A, C, E
Minerals: Calcium, Potassium,
   Iron, Zinc, Magnesium

1 tbsp olive oil
1 large onion, thinly sliced
2 garlic cloves, crushed
2 16-ounce cans crushed tomatoes
   (with liquid)
2 tbsp tomato paste
½ cup dry white wine
1 tbsp red wine vinegar
2 tsp clear honey
1½ cups each drained canned pinto,
   cannellini, and adzuki beans
about 1 cup *Vegetable Stock*
   (see page 122)
salt and black pepper

Heat the oil in a flameproof casserole or large frying pan that has a lid and sauté the onion and garlic until soft.

Add the tomatoes, tomato paste, and wine. Bring to a boil and boil gently 2 minutes.

Stir in the vinegar and honey. Then mix in the beans, stock, and seasoning and simmer very gently for 30 minutes, adding more vegetable stock as necessary to give a rich sauce (the dish shouldn't get too dry).

MACARONI, RED PEPPER, AND BROCCOLI BAKE

To reduce the fat in this dish even further you could use lowfat spread instead of butter in the sauce. However, the fat content here is actually only 21% in total anyway.

Calories per serving: 415
Saturated fat: High
Total fat: Medium
Protein: High
Carbohydrate: High
Cholesterol: 25 mg
Vitamins: A, C, E, B group, D
Minerals: Calcium, Iron,
   Magnesium, Potassium

8 ounces macaroni
1 cup broccoli florets
8 ounces red sweet peppers, seeded
   and cut into ¾-inch sticks
2 tbsp butter
3 tbsp flour
2 cups skim milk
1 cup grated reduced-fat Cheddar
   cheese
salt and black pepper

Preheat the oven to 400°F and grease a baking dish lightly with a little of the butter.

Cook the macaroni in a large pan of boiling salted water until it is tender but still firm to the bite. Drain immediately.

Blanch the broccoli and red sweet pepper in boiling salted water for 3 minutes, drain immediately, and arrange the vegetables and pasta in the baking dish.

Melt the butter in a saucepan and add the flour. Stir and cook over medium heat for 2 minutes. Add the milk and stir until the sauce thickens. Add seasoning and three-quarters of the cheese, and stir again.

Thin the sauce down to a pouring consistency with a little water, then pour it over the pasta and vegetables and top with the remaining cheese.

Bake until the top is brown, about 20 minutes.

SUMMER FRITTATA

Serve this low-calorie – but high-fat – dish with plenty of crusty bread and green salad.

Calories per serving: 200
Saturated fat: High
Total fat: High
Protein: High
Carbohydrate: Low
Cholesterol: 375 mg
Vitamins: A, B group, C, D, E
Minerals: Iron, Potassium, Calcium

1 tbsp corn oil
4 medium zucchini, sliced
1 small sweet red pepper, seeded and thinly sliced
1 garlic clove, chopped
6 medium eggs, lightly beaten
¼ cup chopped sun-dried tomatoes in oil, drained well
6 scallions, trimmed and chopped
1 tbsp chopped fresh basil
1 tbsp chopped fresh mint
salt and black pepper
¼ cup grated reduced-fat Cheddar cheese

Heat the oil in a large nonstick frying pan and cook the zucchini and red pepper until they are fairly soft, about 10 minutes. Add the garlic and stir a minute.

Put the eggs, tomatoes, scallions, herbs, and seasoning in a bowl and mix well. Preheat the broiler.

Reduce the heat under the pan and pour in the egg mixture. Let it run under the vegetables. Cook over low heat until the base of the frittata is golden.

Sprinkle the cheese over the top and place the pan under the broiler until the top is golden.

Serve hot or cold, cut into wedges.

BAKMIE GORENG

This is supposed to be quite a dry stir-fry, but you can add a little vegetable stock toward the end of cooking.

Calories per serving: 325
Saturated fat: Low
Total fat: Medium
Protein: Medium
Carbohydrate: High
Cholesterol: 55 mg
Vitamins: A, B group, C, E
Minerals: Potassium

8 ounces egg-thread noodles
2 tbsp sunflower oil
5 shallots, thinly sliced
8 ounces mixed mushrooms
2 garlic cloves, crushed
2 medium carrots, diced
4 large leaves Napa cabbage, thinly sliced
1 cup mixed beansprouts
2 tomatoes, peeled, seeded, and chopped
4 scallions, chopped
2 tbsp soy sauce
salt and black pepper
chopped parsley for garnish

Soak the noodles according to the package directions.

While the noodles are soaking, heat the oil in a wok or large nonstick frying pan over medium heat and stir-fry the shallots for 2 minutes. Add the mushrooms, garlic, and carrots and fry 2 minutes more. Add the Napa cabbage and stir-fry 1 minute.

Drain the noodles and add them to the pan together with the beansprouts, tomatoes, scallions, soy sauce, and black pepper. Fry until the noodles are hot.

Taste and adjust the seasoning if necessary. Serve immediately, garnished with parsley.

CHANA MASALEDAR

With pita or other flat bread, this makes a good quick supper.

Calories per serving: 157
Saturated fat: Medium
Total fat: Medium
Protein: High
Carbohydrate: High
Cholesterol: None
Vitamins: B group, E
Minerals: Calcium, Iron, Magnesium, Potassium

1¼ tbsp corn or sunflower oil
½ tsp whole cumin seeds
1 medium onion, chopped
1 tsp ground coriander
2 tsp garam masala
piece of fresh gingerroot, minced
pinch of cayenne pepper
1 large garlic clove, crushed
1 tbsp tomato paste
2 cups drained canned chickpeas (liquid reserved)
1 tbsp lemon juice
salt

Heat the oil in a frying pan and add the cumin seeds and onion. Sauté until the onion is soft and barely golden. Reduce the heat and add the rest of the spices and the garlic. Stir a minute or two.

Add the tomato paste, chickpeas, ⅔ cup of the reserved chickpea liquid, and the lemon juice. Stir to blend well, cover, and simmer 30 minutes.

Taste and adjust the seasoning with a little salt if necessary.

THAI-STYLE MIXED VEGETABLES WITH CHILI

You can make this dish as hot or as mild as you like – either way it is tasty and easy to make. I serve it with rice for a filling low-calorie supper.

Calories per serving: 150
Saturated fat: High
Total fat: High
Protein: Medium
Carbohydrate: Low
Cholesterol: None
Vitamins: C, E, Folic acid
Minerals: Potassium

2 tbsp corn oil
1 tbsp coriander seeds, ground
small piece of fresh gingerroot, peeled and chopped
5 hot red chili peppers, seeded and minced, *or* 4 tsp Sambal Oelek paste
7 ounces green beans, cut in half
3½ ounces baby corn
2 cups small cauliflower florets
2 tsp ground turmeric
salt
7 ounces button mushrooms
little *Vegetable Stock* (see page 122)
7 fl oz thick unsweetened coconut milk
1 tsp chopped lemon grass (if dried, soak in water for 15 minutes)
lime juice and lime wedges
2 tsp chopped fresh cilantro

Heat the oil in a wok or heavy frying pan and add the ground coriander seeds, ginger, and chilies or paste. Stir 2 minutes, then add the beans, corn, cauliflower, turmeric, and a little salt. Stir-fry the vegetables for 2 minutes.

Add the whole mushrooms and stir-fry 1 minute. Add a little vegetable stock to prevent sticking, if necessary.

Add the coconut milk and lemon grass with a dash of lime juice. Simmer a minute and serve, garnished with fresh cilantro and lime wedges.

CHINESE EGG AND NOODLE STIR-FRY

This dish is totally delicious and quick to cook, and works just as well if the quantities are reduced to make a one-person supper.

Calories per serving: 420
Saturated fat: Medium
Total fat: Medium
Protein: High
Carbohydrate: Medium
Cholesterol: 300 mg
Vitamins: A, B group, D, E, C
Minerals: iron, Potassium

8 ounces egg-thread noodles
1 tbsp sunflower oil
4 scallions, chopped
1 garlic clove, crushed
piece of fresh gingerroot, peeled and minced
⅓ cup chopped bamboo shoots
2 tbsp sliced water chestnuts
⅓ cup cashew nuts
½ cup button mushrooms
1 tbsp dry sherry
1 cup fresh beansprouts
4 medium eggs, lightly beaten
salt

Soak the noodles according to package directions while you cook the stir-fry.

Heat the oil in a wok or nonstick frying pan and stir-fry the scallions, garlic, and ginger for a minute.

Add the bamboo shoots, water chestnuts, cashew nuts, mushrooms, and sherry and stir a minute. Add the beansprouts, eggs, and salt and cook, stirring, until the eggs are scrambled.

Drain the noodles and serve the stir-fry on them.

DELHI-STYLE CAULIFLOWER

This tasty curry makes a complete meal if you serve it with a lentil or chickpea dhal (see Chana Masaledar *page 77) and some brown or Basmati rice.*

Calories per serving: 155
Saturated fat: Low
Total fat: High
Protein: Medium
Carbohydrate: Medium
Cholesterol: Trace
Vitamins: C
Minerals: Iron

1 tbsp corn or sunflower oil
1 small onion, finely chopped
1 tbsp *Curry Powder* (see page 122)
1 garlic clove
1 pound (about 4 cups) cauliflower
   florets
½ cup green beans, trimmed and cut
   in half
1 tbsp wholewheat flour
1¾ cups *Vegetable Stock*
   (see page 122)
⅓ cup golden raisins
¼ cup sliced almonds
½ cup plain lowfat yogurt
1-inch piece of cucumber, chopped,
   for garnish
fresh cilantro leaves, for garnish

Heat the oil in a frying pan and add the onion. Stir-fry it for a few minutes until soft. Add the curry powder and garlic and stir 2 minutes.

Add the cauliflower and beans. Stir and cook, covered, for a few minutes.

Stir in the flour thoroughly, followed by the stock and raisins. Bring to a simmer, stirring gently, and let simmer, covered, until the cauliflower is just tender, about 12 minutes – don't overcook.

Add the almonds at the last minute. Just before serving, drizzle the yogurt over the dish and garnish with cucumber and cilantro.

FETTUCCINE WITH WINE AND MUSHROOMS

You can use whatever mushrooms you like or can buy, but this dish is improved by having at least two different kinds – although don't use Chinese dried mushrooms.

Calories per serving: 355
Saturated fat: Medium
Total fat: Medium
Protein: Medium
Carbohydrate: High
Cholesterol: 20 mg
Vitamins: A, C, Folic acid,
   Niacin, E
Minerals: Iron, Potassium

8 ounces fettuccine or other flat
   ribbon pasta
1½ tbsp olive oil
1 medium onion, chopped
2 garlic cloves, crushed
1 pound mixed mushrooms
   (e.g. button, yellow oysters, brown
   oysters, shiitake), chopped or torn
1 tbsp butter
1 tbsp flour
about 7 fl oz *Vegetable Stock*
   (see page 122)
¼ cup dry white wine
2 tbsp chopped fresh basil
3 tbsp light cream
salt and black pepper
chopped fresh chives or parsley, for
   garnish
1 tbsp grated Parmesan cheese, for
   garnish

Put the pasta in plenty of lightly salted boiling water together with ½ tablespoon of the oil and boil until just tender, about 10 minutes for dried pasta or 3–5 minutes for fresh.

Heat the remaining oil in a heavy nonstick pan and sauté the onion and garlic until soft and just turning golden. Add the mushrooms and stir. Remove from the heat, but keep the contents of the pan warm.

Melt the butter in a small saucepan, add the flour, and cook 1 minute. Add the stock and wine and bring to a boil. Add the basil and stir until you have a sauce.

Add this sauce to the frying pan and return it to the heat. Add the cream and heat through. Season.

Drain the pasta when it is tender but still firm to the bite. Pour the sauce over and garnish with chives and Parmesan.

TOFU AND VEGETABLE MEDLEY

I find the delicate texture of silken firm tofu nicer in this dish, but you can use ordinary tofu if you like. Serve with a grain of your choice – brown rice and couscous are nice.

Calories per serving: 172
Saturated fat: Low
Total fat: High
Protein: High
Carbohydrate: Low
Cholesterol: None
Vitamins: A, C
Minerals: Calcium, Potassium, Iron

1 tbsp sunflower oil
1 onion, thinly sliced
2 garlic cloves, crushed
2 carrots, cut into julienne strips
2 celery stalks, cut into julienne strips
½ cup green beans, halved
¼ cup sliced water chestnuts
⅔ cup sliced mushrooms
16-ounce can tomatoes
1 cup *Vegetable Stock* (see page 122)
¼ cup light soy sauce
1 tbsp cider vinegar
1 tbsp honey
1 tbsp tomato paste
1 tbsp cornstarch
12 ounces silken firm tofu, cut into strips
1 cup fresh beansprouts

Heat the oil in a flameproof casserole dish, or in a heavy frying pan that has a lid, and fry the onion, garlic, carrots, celery, beans, and water chestnuts for 3 minutes.

Add the mushrooms, tomatoes, stock, soy sauce, vinegar, honey, and tomato paste, stirring well. Bring to a boil, reduce the heat, cover, and simmer 15 minutes.

Mix the cornstarch with 1 tablespoon of water and add to the pan. Stir thoroughly.

Add the strips of tofu and the beansprouts. Stir again gently and serve.

FALAFEL PATTIES

Canned pimiento gives a lovely moist texture to these patties, but you can also use a minced fresh sweet pepper. The patties go marvelously well with pita bread, salad, and **Fresh Tomato Salsa** *or* **Light Mayonnaise** *(see pages 67 and 124).*

Calories per serving: 156
Saturated fat: Medium
Total fat: Medium
Protein: Medium
Carbohydrate: Medium
Cholesterol: 68 mg
Vitamins: C, E
Minerals: Iron

1½ cups dried chickpeas, soaked and cooked as described on page 18, or 15-ounce can, drained
1 small onion, very finely chopped
1 canned pimiento, drained and finely chopped
1 garlic clove, crushed
1 tbsp chopped parsley
1 tsp ground cumin
1 tsp ground coriander
pinch of chili powder
salt and pepper
1 egg, beaten
1 tbsp corn oil
little wholewheat flour for coating

Mash the chickpeas with a fork or put them in a blender to make a coarse purée.

In a bowl, mix the chickpea purée with the onion, pimiento, garlic, parsley, spices, seasoning, and egg. Using your hands, form the mixture into 12 small egg- or sausage-shaped patties.

Heat the oil in a nonstick frying pan. Coat each patty lightly in flour before frying over medium heat until golden, about 10 minutes, turning at least once.

*M*ain courses

*If you have a little time to spare
or feel like trying something
new, these main course
recipes will please both family
and friends.*

My test of a good vegetarian recipe is whether my carnivorous friends find it enjoyable, too. All the recipes in this chapter have been declared successes by all kinds of people: from children to teenagers; from meat-eaters to committed vegetarians.

Few need a great deal of cooking skills, but all have the merit of winning you a reputation as a good "tasty" cook. Not one would be regarded by the anti-health-food brigade as too worthy, yet all can be included in any maintenance or weight-loss diet without guilt. I've reduced the fat content of each to just what is truly necessary, and virtually all provide an abundance of fiber, vitamins, minerals, and protein.

For other main-course ideas, read the Vegetarian Kitchen chapter (page 16). There are also cold main courses in the next chapter, and suppers in the previous chapter that can be "dressed up" a little with the addition of side salads.

Once you have tried these recipes you can confidently begin to experiment with variations of your own. For instance, try baking crêpes stuffed with the Crispy Vegetable Pie filling (page 86), stuff baked vegetables with your own mix of grains, seeds, and vegetables, or mix all kinds of legumes with all kinds of vegetables in casseroles.

Even pastry can form part of a healthy diet. Try the whole-wheat piecrust filled with various vegetables, egg, and some reduced-fat cheese – or use lower-calorie phyllo pastry as a crispy base for a sauté of Mediterranean vegetables.

Rice and grains are an ideal starting point for many a main-course pilaff or risotto – various nuts, seeds, vegetables, stock, and flavorings can give you dozens of different styles of meal with only your imagination to limit you!

Grilled Vegetables with Bulghur (page 84)

CRISPY VEGETABLE PIE

*This delicately flavored
and pretty pie is easy to
make, but does take a
while to assemble. It is
ideal both for family
meals and entertaining.
You will add even more
flavor to this dish if you
have time to preheat the
skim milk slowly, infusing
in it a bay leaf, a chopped
carrot, and some black
peppercorns.*

*Calories per serving: 600 for 4;
    400 for 6*
Saturated fat: Medium
Total fat: Medium
Protein: Medium
Carbohydrate: Medium
Cholesterol: 24 mg
Vitamins: A, C, E
Minerals: Calcium, Potassium

1 large leek, sliced
4 carrots, cubed
1 parsnip, cubed
2 zucchini, cubed
1 small head of broccoli
    (about 4 ounces)
6 tbsp yellow split peas, cooked
    (see chart on page 23)
3 tbsp butter
1½ tbsp flour
7 fl oz skim milk
salt and black pepper
1 tbsp olive oil
6 oblong sheets of phyllo pastry (about
    4 ounces)

Preheat the oven to 375°F .

Cook the leek, carrots, and parsnip in a saucepan of lightly salted water until barely tender. Drain, reserving the cooking water.

In a separate pan of water, cook the zucchini and broccoli for 2 minutes. Drain, then divide the broccoli into small florets.

Arrange the vegetables and split peas in an 11- x 8½-inch ovenproof dish.

Melt 2 tablespoons of the butter in a saucepan and add the flour, stirring a minute or two until you have a thick roux. Gradually add the milk (see left), stirring, until you have a thick sauce. Add 3⅓ cups of the reserved vegetable water and stir. Adjust the seasoning. Pour the sauce evenly over the vegetables.

Melt the remaining butter with the olive oil in a small pan. Making sure that the butter isn't hot, brush each of the first 4 sheets of phyllo pastry and place over the vegetables.

Brush the last 2 sheets with the remaining oil and butter mixture and use each to cover half of the top, gathering into loose folds (rather like drawn curtains). This both looks attractive and gives a much greater "crispy" area when the pie comes out of the oven.

Bake until the top is deep golden brown and crisp, about 25 minutes.

CHEESE AND TOMATO ROULADE

*Roulades are surprisingly
easy to prepare, and make
perfect light summer
dishes if you are dieting.
They can also be used as
first courses for dinner
parties.*

Calories per serving: 225
Saturated fat: High
Total fat: High
Protein: High
Carbohydrate: Low
Cholesterol: 260 mg
Vitamins: A, B group, D, E, C
*Minerals: Calcium, Iron,
    Potassium*

1 tbsp lowfat spread
3 tbsp flour
1 pound fresh ripe tomatoes,
    blanched, peeled, and minced
    (about 2¼ cups)
salt and black pepper
4 eggs, separated
for the filling:
1 cup lowfat cottage cheese
¼ cup nonfat plain yogurt
4 scallions, minced
2 tsp each chopped fresh parsley and
    thyme

Preheat the oven to 375°F. Line a shallow 12- x 8-inch pan with parchment paper.

Melt the spread in a saucepan. Add the flour and cook 1 minute. Stir in the tomatoes and continue to stir 5 minutes. Remove from heat, season, and stir in the egg yolks.

Beat the egg whites to stiff peaks and fold into the tomato mixture. Spoon into the pan and bake until firm, 15-20 minutes.

Meanwhile, prepare the filling: in a bowl, mix the soft cheese and yogurt. Add the scallions, herbs, and some seasoning.

Unmold the roulade. Spread the filling over it and roll it up, removing the parchment paper as you go. Serve warm.

OPPOSITE: Crispy Vegetable Pie; Cheese and Tomato Roulade

CHEESE AND ONION BREAD BAKE

This is a cheese-lover's delight and makes a really robust meal – it needs only a large mixed salad to go with it.

Calories per serving: 450
Saturated fat: High
Total fat: High
Protein: High
Carbohydrate: Medium
Cholesterol: 210 mg
Vitamins: A, B group, C, D, E
Minerals: Calcium, Iron,
    Magnesium, Potassium

1 tbsp corn oil
1 large onion, finely chopped
½ tsp dried thyme
1 cup grated reduced-fat Cheddar
    cheese
¾ cup grated Parmesan cheese
2 tsp chopped fresh chives
8 medium slices of wholewheat bread,
    crusts removed
3 medium eggs
2 cups skim milk
black pepper

Preheat the oven to 375°F and brush an oblong baking dish with a little oil.

Heat the remaining oil in a frying pan and fry the onions with the thyme over low heat, stirring occasionally, until very soft and just turning golden, 15–20 minutes. Mix the cheeses and the chives in a small bowl.

Put 4 slices of bread on the bottom of the prepared dish, ensuring that they fit exactly. Cover with the onion mixture and half the cheese mixture. Put the other slices of bread on top and cover with the remaining cheese.

Whisk the eggs and milk together in a bowl and season with pepper. Pour this over the bread and cheese mixture. Bake until puffed up and golden, about 30 minutes.

MEDITERRANEAN PHYLLO TARTS

This is a very simple dish to make, but it is delicious. Use small tart pans and halve the quantities to make a delightful first course.

If using Haloumi cheese, which isn't as salty as Feta, you might like to add a little sea salt.

There are several variations you can try with this dish: for a lighter course, you could omit the avocado; Spanish canned piquillo peppers are a tasty and easy substitute for the broiled red bell peppers – allow 2 per person, and drain well.

Calories per serving: 325
Saturated fat: Medium
Total fat: Medium
Protein: Medium
Carbohydrate: Low
Cholesterol: 22 mg
Vitamins: A, C, D, E
Minerals: Calcium

4 red sweet peppers, seeded and
    quartered
8 sheets of phyllo pastry, cut into 16
    5-inch squares (discard any surplus)
1 tbsp olive oil
3½ ounces Feta or Haloumi cheese, cut
    into small squares
4 juicy black olives, pitted and
    chopped
⅔ cup chopped just-ripe avocado,
    (chop at the last minute)
2 medium scallions, sliced into thin
    rounds
1 tbsp olive oil
black pepper
4 fresh basil leaves, chopped, for
    garnish (optional)

Preheat the broiler. Place the sweet peppers on a nonstick baking sheet, skin-side up, and broil until the skins are black.

Place the peppers in a plastic bag and cool 15 minutes, then peel off the skins and cut the flesh into diamond shapes.

Preheat the oven to 350°F.

Line 4 individual metal tart pans with the phyllo sheets, each one very lightly brushed with oil (it doesn't matter if the oil doesn't cover all of each sheet). Arrange 4 sheets in each pan so that you have an even eight-pointed star shape.

Place the lined pans on a baking sheet and bake until the pastry is a very light golden brown, about 6 minutes. Leaving the oven on, remove the pastry shells and let cool for a minute, then remove from the pans.

While the shells are cooling, combine the remaining ingredients, except the basil if using, in a bowl. Divide among the pastry shells, making sure several pieces of cheese are visible on the top of each filling. Grind a little black pepper on top of each and garnish with a little basil if you have it.

Warm in the oven until the cheese pieces are turning golden at the edges, about 10 minutes, then serve immediately.

OPPOSITE: Delhi-Style Cauliflower (page 80); Mediterranean Phyllo Tarts

MUSHROOM PILAF

For a change, try replacing half the mushrooms with cèpes or other wild mushrooms to make this tasty dish even tastier. You can buy them dried and reconstitute them by soaking them in water.

Calories per serving: 400
Saturated fat: Low
Total fat: Medium
Protein: Low
Carbohydrate: High
Cholesterol: None
Vitamins: B, E
Minerals: Potassium

2 tbsp corn or olive oil
1 onion, finely chopped
1 small red sweet pepper, seeded and
   finely chopped
1½ cups brown rice (ordinary or
   instant)
1½ cups chopped mushrooms
2½ cups *Vegetable Stock*
   (see page 122)
salt and black pepper
2 tbsp chopped fresh parsley
2½ tbsp sunflower seeds
¼ cup sliced almonds

Heat half the oil in a nonstick frying pan and sauté the onion over medium heat until soft and just turning golden. Add the rest of the oil and the sweet pepper and stir 2 minutes. Add the rice and stir again.

Add the mushrooms, stock, seasoning, and half the parsley and bring to a boil. Lower the heat, cover the pan, and simmer 20 minutes if using instant rice or up to 45 minutes if using ordinary, adding more stock from time to time if necessary.

About 5 minutes before the end of cooking time, stir in the seeds and nuts. When the rice is tender and virtually all the liquid has been absorbed, serve the pilaf sprinkled with the remaining parsley.

TOFU KEBABS WITH PEANUT SAUCE

Although low in calories, this dish is reasonably high in fat; serve it with plenty of grain – e.g. Thai fragrant rice – to make the complete meal low in fat.

Calories per serving: 240
Saturated fat: Medium
Total fat: High
Protein: High
Carbohydrate: Low
Cholesterol: Trace
Vitamins: A, C, E
Minerals: Calcium, Potassium,
   Iron, Zinc

2 carrots
2 medium zucchini
12 ounces smoked tofu, cubed
3 small red onions
1 small garlic clove
1 tbsp olive oil
salt and black pepper
2 tsp soybean or corn oil
3 tbsp crunchy peanut butter
2 tsp light brown sugar
2 tsp light soy sauce
¼ cup skim milk

Preheat the broiler.

Using a vegetable peeler, cut the carrots and zucchini down their lengths into thin ribbons. Wrap these around the cubes of tofu. Quarter two of the onions.

Thread the tofu cubes and onion on soaked wooden kebab sticks or metal skewers.

Crush the garlic and mash it into the olive oil with some black pepper and a very little salt. Brush this over the kebabs and place under the broiler for about 10 minutes, turning several times.

Meanwhile make the sauce: mince the remaining onion, heat the soybean oil in a nonstick saucepan, and sauté the onion until golden. Stir in the peanut butter, sugar, and soy sauce. Gradually add 7 tablespoons water over medium heat, stirring. Finally, mix in the milk.

When the kebabs are golden, serve them with the peanut sauce.

Salads and vegetable accompaniments

Salads and vegetables are almost as versatile within the vegetarian diet as soups and appetizers – and even more essential. So here are plenty of ideas with which to begin.

As so many vegetarian "main courses" already contain vegetables, vegetarians often don't pay a lot of attention to serving side salads and vegetable accompaniments. This is a pity, as lightly cooked or raw vegetables are important in the vegetarian diet, because as well as being generally rich in vitamins and minerals they are the best source – apart from fresh fruit – of vitamin C. This vitamin is depleted when it is heated and cooked, especially in a casserole or baked dish that has a long cooking time. Health considerations apart, side vegetables also add variety, visual appeal, and filling power for only a few extra calories.

This chapter provides both hot and cold vegetable side dishes that best complement the main courses in the previous chapter and will go well with all kinds of bakes, loaves, etc. You can create your own side salads from seasonal vegetables and herbs and, if you like, add a little fresh or dried fruit or a sprinkling of nuts or seeds. It is easy to make a side dish look and taste impressive.

However, don't turn your nose up at plainly cooked vegetables or leaf salads. If you have a rich main course, there is nothing quite so delicious as a lightly steamed, boiled, or roasted vegetable served with nothing more than a little black pepper or a very light drizzle of olive oil, or a freshly picked lettuce tossed with a little balsamic vinegar.

I've also given some recipes for more substantial salads suitable as a meal in themselves for a lunch or supper or, in half portions, as appetizers. You can even convert some of the side dishes into more hearty dishes; for instance, you could mix the Fruit Coleslaw with a handful of hazelnuts and serve this with some bread for a light lunch.

Always buy vegetables as fresh as possible, nearing their peak; store them in cool, dark conditions, and never overcook them!

Eggplant and Lentil Layer (page 84);
Endive, Orange, and Date Salad (page 103)

CANTONESE NOODLE SALAD

Try white rice noodles in this dish for a change from the more commonly available wheat-based ones.

Calories per serving: 235
Saturated fat: Low
Total fat: Medium
Protein: Medium
Carbohydrate: High
Cholesterol: 25 mg
Vitamins: A, C, E
Minerals: Iron

4 ounces egg-thread noodles
3½ ounces snow peas, trimmed and
   halved
1½ cups fresh beansprouts
½ cup alfalfa sprouts
6 scallions, cut into ¾-inch pieces
1 large red sweet pepper, seeded and
   chopped
1¼ cups sliced Napa cabbage
1½ cups sliced mushrooms
for the dressing:
1 tbsp soy sauce
2 tbsp lemon juice
1 tbsp sesame oil
pinch of ground ginger
1 tbsp sesame seeds
1 tbsp sunflower seeds

Soak the noodles in boiling water for a few minutes, and blanch the snow peas for 1 minute in boiling salted water. Drain immediately.

Combine all the vegetables in a salad bowl. In another small bowl, mix together the dressing ingredients.

Drain the noodles and add them to the salad bowl together with the dressing. Stir gently to combine, and serve.

HOT BABY VEGETABLES WITH RED PESTO

Calories per serving: 208
Saturated fat: High
Total fat: High
Protein: High
Carbohydrate: Medium
Cholesterol: 11 mg
Vitamins: C, A
Minerals: Potassium, Iron,
   Calcium

10 ounces very small new potatoes,
   scrubbed
8 ounces baby carrots
6 ounces baby summer squash
8 shallots, peeled and sliced
3 ounces baby asparagus spears,
   trimmed
3 ounces fine green beans, trimmed,
   or ¾ cup broccoli florets
1 quantity *Red Pesto Sauce* (see *Pistou*
   on page 53)

Cook the potatoes in boiling salted water until tender. Meanwhile, in a steamer (preferably one with compartments), steam the other vegetables until just tender, about 10 minutes (or you could microwave them in a little water).

When the vegetables are ready, quickly toss with the sauce in a serving dish and serve.
Note: if young asparagus is too expensive, substitute snow peas.

CLASSIC THREE-BEAN SALAD WITH PASTA

Calories per serving: 347
Saturated fat: Low
Total fat: Medium
Protein: High
Carbohydrate: High
Cholesterol: None
Vitamins: B group, C, E
Minerals: Calcium, Iron,
   Potassium, Magnesium

5 ounces (about 1 cup) pasta shells
7 ounces green beans, trimmed
1 cup drained canned or cooked (see
   pages 22–23) cannellini beans
1 cup drained canned or cooked (see
   pages 22–23) red kidney beans
6 tbsp *Light Vinaigrette* (see page 124)
2 tbsp chopped fresh parsley

Cook the pasta in plenty of lightly salted water with a little oil until it is tender but still firm to the bite.

Cook the green beans in lightly salted water for a few minutes until they are tender but still crunchy.

Drain the pasta and beans and mix with the remaining ingredients in a serving bowl.
Note: this serves 4 as a lunch or 8 as an appetizer – in this latter case it will provide 173 calories per serving.

OPPOSITE: Cantonese Noodle Salad

GADO GADO

This warm salad from Indonesia provides one of the nicest combinations of tastes and textures I've ever enjoyed. It is a bit of an effort to put together, but well worth the trouble.

Calories per serving: 273
Saturated fat: High
Total fat: High
Protein: High
Carbohydrate: Low
Cholesterol: 250 mg
Vitamins: A, B group, C, D, E
Minerals: Iron, Potassium, Zinc,
*   Magnesium, Calcium*

1⅓ cups Napa cabbage, torn into large pieces
1½ cups cooked potatoes cut into bite-sized pieces
1 cup carrots cut into thick strips, blanched in boiling water for 1 minute and drained immediately
1 cup green beans cut in half, blanched in boiling water for 1 minute and drained immediately
½ tbsp corn oil
⅓ cup cucumber cut into thick strips
1 cup fresh beansprouts
4 medium eggs, hard-boiled and quartered
1 small onion, sliced and separated into rings
for the sauce:
¼ cup unsweetened coconut cream
2 tbsp smooth peanut butter
2 tsp lime juice
2 tsp light soy sauce
1 tsp hot pepper sauce

Mix the sauce ingredients together and set aside.

Line 4 serving dishes with the Napa cabbage and divide the cooked vegetables among the dishes, arranging them attractively.

Heat the oil in a small nonstick frying pan and stir-fry the cucumber and beansprouts over high heat until crisp-tender, 1-2 minutes. Sprinkle these on the vegetables and dot with the quartered eggs.

Add the onion to the pan and stir-fry until it is crisp and golden. Pour the dressing over the salad and top with the onion for garnish.

The salad should still be slightly warm when served, so the vegetables are best cooked just before you arrange the salads.

PASTA WALDORF

You can serve half portions of this dish as an appetizer if people are very hungry, or give yourself a half portion with some bread if you're dieting. Otherwise, this is a really hearty main-course dish.

Calories per serving: 430
Saturated fat: Low
Total fat: Medium
Protein: Medium
Carbohydrate: High
Cholesterol: 5 mg
Vitamins: A, B group, D, C
Minerals: Calcium, Potassium,
*   Iron*

8 ounces (about 1½ cups) pasta shells
3 small red apples
1 tbsp lemon juice
6 celery stalks, chopped
½ cup walnut pieces
⅓ cup golden raisins
½ cup reduced-fat Cheddar cheese cut into small cubes
for the dressing:
1 quantity *Light Mayonnaise* (see page 124)
about 3 tbsp skim milk
curly endive leaves, for serving (optional)
2 tbsp chopped fresh parsley, for garnish

Cook the pasta in boiling salted water until tender. Drain and let cool.

Core, seed, and dice the apples and toss them in the lemon juice.

Combine all the salad ingredients in a salad bowl or on a platter lined with curly endive leaves.

Make the dressing by adding just enough of the skim milk to the mayonnaise to give it a pouring consistency.

Drizzle the dressing over the salad and toss lightly to ensure that all the ingredients are evenly coated. Sprinkle the parsley over for garnish.

BROWN RICE SALAD
WITH MUSHROOMS AND BEANS

I prefer the nutty taste of brown rice in this salad, but you could use Basmati or even soaked bulghur wheat.

Calories per serving: 395
Saturated fat: Low
Total fat: Medium
Protein: Medium
Carbohydrate: High
Cholesterol: None
Vitamins: B group, C, A, E
Minerals: Iron, Potassium, Zinc

1¼ cups brown rice, washed and drained
1¼ cups drained canned or cooked (see pages 22–3) cannellini beans
⅔ cup each drained canned or cooked (see pages 22–3) borlotti and adzuki beans
1½ cups sliced mushrooms
1 medium red sweet pepper, seeded and chopped
2 celery stalks, chopped
⅓ cup chopped cucumber
6 scallions, chopped
1 small red apple, chopped
¼ cup *Light Vinaigrette* (see page 124)

Cook the rice in 2¾ cups boiling salted water until tender, and all the water is absorbed, about 30 minutes (add extra water during cooking at any time if the rice dries out but still isn't tender). Let cool slightly.

Combine the rice with all the other ingredients in a salad bowl, mix well, and serve.

AVOCADO AND LEAF SALAD

Avocados are high in fat, but quite low in saturates and high in the "good-for-you" monounsaturates.

Calories per serving: 290
Saturated fat: Medium
Total fat: High
Protein: Medium
Carbohydrate: Low
Cholesterol: None
Vitamins: A, C, E
Minerals: Potassium, Iron, Calcium

1 tomato
1 pound mixed salad leaves, including some dark leaves
1 bunch of watercress, trimmed and separated
4 large scallions, chopped
2 medium-to-small ripe avocados
2 tbsp *Light Vinaigrette* (see page 124)
⅓ cup pine nuts

Quarter the tomato, seed it, and roughly chop it. Put the leaves in a serving bowl with the tomato, watercress, and scallions.

Halve, seed, and peel the avocados. Slice the flesh and add it to the salad. Immediately pour the dressing over and gently toss to mix.

Sprinkle the salad with the pine nuts before serving. This salad is delicious as a light lunch with sesame rolls.

APPLE, NUT, AND CARROT SALAD

Calories per serving: 203
Saturated fat: Medium
Total fat: High
Protein: Medium
Carbohydrate: Low
Cholesterol: None
Vitamins: C, A, E
Minerals: Potassium, Iron

2 red apples
1 tbsp lemon juice
3 cups peeled and grated carrots
3 tbsp cashew nuts
1½ tbsp sunflower seeds
2 tbsp chopped walnuts
⅓ cup raisins
3 tbsp *Light Vinaigrette* (see page 124)

Core and slice the apples and sprinkle with lemon juice.

Combine all the ingredients in a salad bowl and mix well.

Note: half portions of this salad make good side salads, while a whole portion makes a very big appetizer or light lunch.

FRUIT COLESLAW

This slaw is good as part of a buffet, and in sandwiches with cheese or one of the spreads on pages 63–6.

½ small head of white cabbage (about 12 ounces)
¾ cup small seedless grapes
2½ tbsp dried shredded coconut
⅔ cup diced fresh pineapple
¼ cup *Light Mayonnaise* (see page 124)
2 tbsp lowfat plain yogurt

Slice the cabbage thinly, then chop it into 1¼-inch lengths and put these into a salad bowl. Halve the grapes and mix them into the cabbage together with the coconut and pineapple.

Combine the light mayonnaise with the yogurt and pour this dressing over the salad. Toss lightly to mix, and chill before serving.
Note: you can add extra ingredients to this salad as you like: e.g. grated carrots or onions, chopped apple, or fresh apricots.

Calories per serving: 106
Saturated fat: Medium
Total fat: Medium
Protein: Medium
Carbohydrate: Medium
Cholesterol: 10 mg
Vitamins: C
Minerals: Potassium

ENDIVE, ORANGE, AND DATE SALAD

1 large orange
2 heads of Belgian endive, sliced
4½ tbsp chopped dried dates
3 tbsp oil-free French dressing

Peel the orange, removing all the pith. Segment it with a sharp serrated knife.

Mix all the ingredients together in a salad bowl. This goes well with cheese and any bake or nut loaf.
Note: you can use 3 ounces fresh dates instead, which will provide a slightly different texture. You can also vary the salad by using the oil-free Vinegar Dressing on page 125.

Calories per serving: 46
Saturated fat: Low
Total fat: Low
Protein: Medium
Carbohydrate: High
Cholesterol: None
Vitamins: C, Folic acid
Minerals: Iron, Potassium, Calcium

WINTER RED SALAD

1 head of red leaf lettuce (about 3½ ounces)
1 head of radicchio
1 cup cooked diced beets
1 red onion, thinly sliced
1½ cups shredded red cabbage
¼ cup *Light Vinaigrette* (see page 124)
2 tsp sesame seeds

Separate the lettuce and radicchio into leaves and tear the bigger ones. Carefully clean and dry the leaves if necessary.

Put all ingredients except the seeds in a salad bowl and toss lightly. Garnish with the sesame seeds.
Note: this salad looks very pretty and goes well with all kinds of cheese.

Calories per serving: 110
Saturated fat: High
Total fat: High
Protein: Medium
Carbohydrate: Low
Cholesterol: None
Vitamins: A, C, Folic acid
Minerals: Potassium

ORANGE AND WATERCRESS SALAD

1 bunch of watercress, trimmed
2 oranges, peeled, pith removed, and thinly sliced into rounds
⅓ cup chopped dried apricots
1 tbsp lemon juice
1 tsp chopped lemon grass, soaked and drained if not fresh
sprigs of fresh herbs, for garnish

Arrange the watercress on the bottom of a shallow serving bowl.

Arrange the orange slices and apricots on top and sprinkle with the lemon juice and lemon grass.

Garnish with a few sprigs of fresh herbs.
Note: this tangy salad is excellent with any rich quiche or bread.

Calories per serving: 53
Saturated fat: Low
Total fat: Low
Protein: Low
Carbohydrate: High
Cholesterol: None
Vitamins: C, A
Minerals: Iron, Potassium

GUMBO CREOLE

Use as a side vegetable, or add some cubes of tofu and serve with a grain or pasta for a main meal.

Calories per serving: 86
Saturated fat: Medium
Total fat: High
Protein: High
Carbohydrate: Medium
Cholesterol: None
Vitamins: A, C, Folic acid, E
Minerals: Iron, Potassium,
*   Calcium, Magnesium*

1 tbsp sunflower oil
1 medium onion, chopped
8 ounces okra, trimmed and cut in half
1 red and 1 green sweet pepper,
    seeded and sliced
1 celery stalk, chopped
16-ounce can crushed tomatoes
1 tbsp tomato paste
1¼ cups *Vegetable Stock*
    (see page 122)
½ tsp chili powder
salt and black pepper

Heat the oil in a medium flameproof casserole dish and sauté the onion gently for 5 minutes. Add the okra and sweet peppers and sauté 10 minutes longer. Add the celery and stir a minute. Stir in the tomatoes and tomato paste.

Add the stock and chili powder. Bring to a simmer, reduce the heat, and cover. Simmer until the okra is tender and the gumbo is thick, about 45 minutes.

Season to taste before serving.

LEMON AND GARLIC ROASTED POTATOES

Cook these in the oven with any bake or loaf.

Calories per serving: 225
Saturated fat: Low
Total fat: Low
Protein: Medium
Carbohydrate: High
Cholesterol: None
Vitamins: C
Minerals: Potassium

2 pounds new potatoes, scrubbed
2 large garlic cloves, chopped
juice of ½ lemon
1 tbsp olive oil
1 tbsp chopped fresh thyme
salt and black pepper
thyme sprigs and strips of lemon peel
    for garnish (optional)

Preheat the oven to 400°F.

Cut larger potatoes into fairly small chunks and toss with the rest of the ingredients.

Spread them out in a roasting pan and pour over any remaining juices. Roast 45 minutes, turning and basting once or twice.

Garnish with thyme sprigs and strips of lemon peel, if using.

Note: instead of adding the garlic chopped, try roasting some whole unpeeled garlic cloves with the potatoes to squeeze over them at the table.

FRIED PEPPERS WITH TOMATO AND GARLIC

These are lovely with any egg dish. Mixed with grated cheese, they also make a good quick supper.

Calories per serving: 65
Saturated fat: Medium
Total fat: High
Protein: Medium
Carbohydrate: None
Cholesterol: 10 mg
Vitamins: A, C, E
Minerals: Potassium

1 tbsp olive oil
1 medium onion, finely chopped
1 large garlic clove, chopped
1 large red and 1 large green sweet
    pepper, seeded and thinly sliced
2 tsp chopped fresh oregano
1 cup canned crushed tomatoes (with
    their liquid)
salt and black pepper

Heat the oil in a nonstick frying pan and sauté the onion over medium heat until soft and just turning golden.

Stir in the garlic and sweet peppers and fry 15 minutes more, adding a little juice from the tomatoes if necessary.

Add the oregano, tomatoes, and seasoning. Cover and simmer 10 minutes, stirring once or twice.

Note: you can let this simmer very gently for much longer if you have the time – it seems to improve the flavor even further.

OPPOSITE: Lemon and Garlic Roasted Potatoes

Sweet treats and breakfasts

Desserts, cakes, cookies, scones, and muffins are just some of the indulgences you can enjoy without feeling guilty by means of the reduced-fat, reduced-sugar recipes in this chapter.

Many a vegetarian's downfall in the quest for a healthy diet is a sweet tooth – which will never quite be satisfied by fresh fruit.

There are two ways of fitting desserts into a healthy and non-fattening diet. One is to exercise extreme restraint in both portion-size and frequency – which is fine if you can do it. The other is to find ways to produce results just as tempting as the high-calorie equivalents, but which contain less fat, less sugar, and fewer calories.

One of the best ways to reduce sugar content is to make use of fruit's own natural sweetness (as in, say, the Peach and Raisin Cookies on page 111), so that added sugar can be reduced. I have also substituted fructose (fruit sugar) for ordinary sugar where appropriate, as it is twice as sweet for the same number of calories.

The last reason you shouldn't feel guilty about indulging in my sweets is that they are all rich in vitamins and minerals – and most contain a lot of fiber.

When making your own desserts, remember that those based on fruit are preferable to heavy puddings and pastries. However, if you do like a "real" dessert, bread is a better bet than pastry – summer puddings and charlottes made with all kinds of fruit fillings are delicious, filling, and healthy. Phyllo is another good choice, as it is far less caloric than other pastries. Use the Phyllo Tarts recipe on page 90 and fill them with chopped fresh fruit and lowfat cottage cheese, then drizzle a little honey on top.

Breakfast can also be a happy blend of indulging a sweet tooth and getting a really healthy start to the day. All the breakfast recipes here achieve that – and for more healthy morning meal ideas, turn to the diet plans starting on pages 35 and 45.

Summer Pudding (page 108)

SUMMER PUDDING

This tastes deceptively wicked, but it is actually a vitamin- and fiber-rich lowfat wonder! It is really nice served with thick plain yogurt or crème fraîche.

Calories per serving: 180 to serve 4; 120 to serve 6
Saturated fat: Low
Total fat: Low
Protein: Medium
Carbohydrate: High
Cholesterol: None
Vitamins: C
Minerals: Iron, Calcium

2 pounds mixed soft fruits (e.g. raspberries, blackberries, and red currants), hulled
about 3 tbsp fructose
6 large slices of bread (white or wholewheat), crusts removed (about 6 ounces)

Put all the fruits in a saucepan with a very little water and the fructose. Bring slowly to a simmer, then remove from the heat and adjust sweetness if necessary.

Line a 5-cup pudding bowl or other domed mold with most of the bread, making sure there are no gaps. Fill the lined bowl with the fruit and most of the juice. Top with the rest of the bread to cover completely, trimming as necessary.

Put a plate on top of the pudding and a heavy weight (such as a can of food) on top of that. Put the bowl on a large plate (because some juices will probably run out of the bowl). Leave overnight in the refrigerator. Keep the remaining juice in a jar in the refrigerator.

When ready to serve, remove the weight and covering plate and slide a spatula around the inside of the bowl to release the pudding. Unmold onto a serving plate, cut the pudding into slices with a carving knife, and pour the extra juice over.

BAKED BANANAS WITH LEMON AND ORANGE

Calories per serving: 110
Saturated fat: None
Total fat: Low
Protein: Low
Carbohydrate: High
Cholesterol: None
Vitamins: C, Folic acid
Minerals: Potassium

4 bananas
juice of 1 lemon
juice of 1 orange, plus 4 slices of orange, peeled and trimmed with a knife
1 tbsp dark brown sugar

Preheat the oven to 350°F.

Peel the bananas and arrange them on 4 pieces of foil large enough to wrap the bananas comfortably. Sprinkle with the citrus juices and sugar and top each with an orange slice.

Wrap the foil into loose packages and tightly seal the edges. Bake 20 minutes.

Serve the bananas in the foil packages.

BAKED PEACHES

Calories per serving: 93
Saturated fat: High
Total fat: Medium
Protein: Low
Carbohydrate: High
Cholesterol: 8 mg
Vitamins: C
Minerals: Trace

4 ripe peaches
1 tbsp brown sugar
1 tbsp lemon juice
1 tbsp butter or vegetarian margarine

Preheat the oven to 350°F.

Cut off a thin layer of flesh from the top and base of each peach and set the peaches in a baking dish. Sprinkle the sugar and lemon juice over them, dot with butter, and bake 20 minutes.

Note: these are lovely with vanilla ice cream.

CARIBBEAN CAKE

You won't keep this around long once it's made, and it is so good for you it is almost saintly!

Makes about 18 slices
Calories per 50 g / 2 ounces
*   slice: 155*
Saturated fat: Low
Total fat: High
Protein: Medium
Carbohydrate: Medium
Cholesterol: 27 mg per slice
Vitamins: A, B group, D, E
Minerals: Iron, Potassium,
*   Magnesium, Zinc*

1½ cups cubed sweet potato (the orange-fleshed variety)
¾ cup packed dark brown sugar
¾ cup + 2 tbsp wholewheat flour
pinch of ground cinnamon
1 tsp grated nutmeg
6 tbsp sunflower oil
2 medium eggs, separated
1 tsp baking soda mixed with 3 tbsp water
½ tsp vanilla extract
½ cup + 1 tbsp chopped almonds
½ cup dried shredded coconut

Preheat the oven to 350°F.

Cook the sweet potato in a very little water until tender, about 10 minutes. Add half of the sugar (without draining any surplus water away) and purée. Reserve.

In a large bowl, combine the flour, remaining sugar, cinnamon, and nutmeg. Make a well in the center and stir in the oil, egg yolks, soda mixture, and vanilla. Fold in the nuts, sweet potato, and coconut.

Beat the egg whites until they form stiff peaks and fold into the mixture.

Pour into a large nonstick loaf pan and bake until cooked, about 1¼ hours.

Let cool slightly, then unmold onto a rack to cool completely.

REDUCED-FAT SCONES

Those of you with a sweet tooth can eat these scones without feeling guilty.

Makes 8
Calories per scone: 150
Saturated fat: Medium
Total fat: Medium
Protein: Medium
Carbohydrate: High
Cholesterol: Not known
Vitamins: B group
Minerals: Zinc

1 cup + 2 tbsp wholewheat flour
⅓ cup all-purpose flour
1 tbsp baking powder
little salt
¼ cup sugar
¼ cup lowfat spread
6 tbsp skim milk

Preheat the oven to 400°F with a nonstick baking sheet in it.

Sift the flours, baking powder, and salt into a mixing bowl and add any flour left in the sifter to the mixing bowl.

Add the sugar and stir in. Cut the lowfat spread into the flour until the mixture resembles fine bread crumbs. Add the milk to make a dough that comes away cleanly from the sides of the bowl.

Either cut 8 rounds from the rolled-out dough, or form it into a 6-inch round and mark that into 8 triangles. Put on the preheated baking sheet and bake 15 minutes.

LEMON AND LIME SORBET

This is a really easy and refreshing dessert.

Calories per serving: 162
Saturated fat: Low
Total fat: Low
Protein: Low
Carbohydrate: High
Cholesterol: None
Vitamins: C
Minerals: Trace

¾ cup sugar
½ cup fresh lemon juice
½ cup fresh lime juice
2 egg whites

Dissolve the sugar in 1½ cups water over low heat, stirring. Bring to a boil and boil 10 minutes. Let cool.

Add the lemon and lime juices. Pour the mixture into a plastic dish and freeze until mushy. Turn into a large mixing bowl and whisk until frothy.

In another bowl beat the egg whites until they form stiff peaks. Fold them into the juice mixture. Put back in the plastic dish and freeze until firm.

Move to the refrigerator a few minutes before eating, to let the sorbet soften slightly.

HAZELNUT ICE CREAM

This is an easy way to enliven vanilla ice cream.

Calories per serving: 160
Saturated fat: Medium
Total fat: Medium
Protein: Medium
Carbohydrate: Low
Cholesterol: None
Vitamins: B
Minerals: Iron, Calcium

½ cup stale wholewheat bread crumbs
3 tbsp brown sugar
3 tbsp finely chopped roasted
  hazelnuts
1 tsp ground cinnamon
½ tsp ground apple pie spice
1 pint low-calorie vanilla ice cream,
  slightly softened

Preheat the oven to 375°F.

Combine the bread crumbs, sugar, and nuts and spread the mixture on a baking sheet. Bake 5–10 minutes until crunchy (check from time to time, as the mixture burns easily.)

Remove from the oven and mix in the spices. Then quickly fold the mixture into the ice cream. Return the ice cream to a plastic container and freeze briefly to firm it up again.

PEACH AND RAISIN COOKIES

This is a moist, cake-like cookie.

Makes 20 big cookies
Calories per cookie: 145
Saturated fat: Medium
Total fat: Medium
Protein: High
Carbohydrate: High
Cholesterol: 12 mg per cookie
Vitamins: A, Folic acid, D
Minerals: Iron, Potassium,
  Calcium, Zinc

1⅔ cups wholewheat flour
1 tsp salt
1 tsp baking powder
pinch of baking soda
½ tsp ground cinnamon
⅓ cup rolled oats
½ cup lowfat spread
1 cup packed light brown sugar
1 egg, beaten
⅔ cup skim milk
⅔ cup chopped dried peaches
⅔ cup raisins
2 tsp finely grated orange zest

Preheat the oven to 400°F.

Sift the flour, salt, baking powder, soda, and cinnamon together into a mixing bowl, and add any flour left in the sifter to the bowl. Add the oats and stir.

Cream the lowfat spread and sugar in another bowl. Beat the egg with the milk.

Add these dry and wet ingredient mixtures alternately to the sugar mixture, stirring each addition in well. Finally, add the peaches, raisins, and orange zest.

Drop tablespoons of the cookie dough onto a nonstick baking sheet, allowing at least ¾–1¼ inches between them. Bake 15 minutes. Let cool and then store in an airtight container.

MARINATED STRAWBERRIES

Serve this easy dessert or breakfast with lowfat cottage cheese or plain yogurt.

Calories per serving: 55
Saturated fat: None
Total fat: Low
Protein: Low
Carbohydrate; High
Cholesterol: None
Vitamins: C
Minerals: Potassium

1 pound ripe strawberries, hulled
juice of 1 large orange
juice of 1 lime, plus lime slices
1 tbsp fructose
1 tsp arrowroot mixed with
  2 tsp cold water
mint leaves, for garnish

Halve all but 4 of the strawberries. Put the strawberry halves and whole strawberries in a shallow bowl.

Mix the citrus juices and fructose with tablespoons water. Pour over the strawberries and let marinate in the refrigerator for about 30 minutes, turning the strawberries once.

Drain the marinade into a small saucepan, add the arrowroot mixture, and stir over medium heat until the mixture bubbles and thickens.

Arrange the strawberry halves in 4 serving dishes and pour the sauce over. Garnish each with a whole strawberry and some mint leaves.

BANANA AND WALNUT BREAD

Makes about 12 slices
Calories per slice: 115
Saturated fat: Medium
Total fat: High
Protein: Medium
Carbohydrate: Medium
Cholesterol: 4 mg per slice
Vitamins: A, B, D
Minerals: Iron

⅓ cup vegetarian margarine
¼ cup packed dark brown sugar
1 medium banana
2 eggs, beaten
⅔ cup + 1 tbsp wholewheat flour
1 medium carrot, peeled, chopped,
  and puréed in blender or very finely
  grated
¼ cup chopped walnuts

Preheat the oven to 350°F.

In a mixing bowl, blend together the margarine and sugar until creamy. Mash the banana and blend this into the mixture.

Add the eggs little by little (to prevent curdling, add a very little flour as you beat in the egg). Add the carrot and nuts and mix well. Add the rest of the flour.

Spread the batter evenly in a small nonstick loaf pan and bake 30 minutes. Let cool on a rack.

PINEAPPLE MUFFINS

These quick muffins make a delicious breakfast.

Makes 8
Calories per serving: 185
Saturated fat: Medium
Total fat: Medium
Protein: Medium
Carbohydrate: High
Cholesterol: Not known
Vitamins: A, D, E
Minerals: Iron, Potassium,
  Calcium

1½ cups self-rising wholewheat flour
pinch of salt
1 medium apple
⅔ cup diced fresh pineapple
⅔ cup skim milk
¼ cup lowfat spread
¼ cup packed brown sugar
2 medium eggs, beaten

Preheat the oven to 375°F.

Sift the flour and salt into a mixing bowl and add any flour left in the sifter to the bowl. Peel, core, and grate the apple.

Stir all the ingredients into the flour gradually until you have a smooth mixture. Pour into muffin pans and bake 20–25 minutes.

Let cool slightly before unmolding onto a wire rack.

OPPOSITE: Marinated Strawberries; Banana and Walnut Bread

APRICOT AND BRANDY SPREAD

The brandy in this spread is not just there to give a luxurious taste for a few calories – it helps to preserve the spread, which will keep for a week or two in an airtight container in the refrigerator.

⅔ cup chopped dried apricots
2 tbsp golden raisins
1 tbsp honey
1 tbsp brandy

Put the apricots in a saucepan with 7 fl oz water and bring to a boil. Remove any scum that rises.

After simmering for 5 minutes, add the raisins and honey. As the mixture thickens, add the brandy and simmer 3 minutes longer.

Let cool and purée in a blender.

Note: this quantity gives four very generous servings.

Calories per serving: 77
Saturated fat: Low
Total fat: Low
Protein: Medium
Carbohydrate: High
Cholesterol: None
Vitamins: A, B2
Minerals: Magnesium, Iron, Calcium

BANANA SPREAD

Calories per serving: 112
Saturated fat: Low
Total fat: Medium
Protein: Medium
Carbohydrate: High
Cholesterol: None
Vitamins: A, C
Minerals: Potassium

3 medium bananas
2 tsp lemon juice
6 tbsp ground almonds
2 tsp brown sugar

Peel the bananas and mash them in a bowl with the lemon juice. Add the almonds and sugar and mix thoroughly.

This makes a good sandwich filling, or a sweet dip for strawberries or slices of apple.

Note: if you like you can use sliced almonds and purée the mixture in a blender for a few seconds.

SCOTTISH OATCAKES

These go well with a variety of things, making a good portable snack or breakfast.

Makes 18
Calories per oatcake: 78
Saturated fat: Medium
Total fat: High
Protein: Medium
Carbohydrate: High
Cholesterol: None
Vitamins: B group, A
Minerals: Iron, Potassium

2¾ cups rolled oats
⅓ cup wholewheat flour
1 tsp baking powder
¼ cup polyunsaturated margarine
little salt
little boiling water
little flour for dusting

Preheat the oven to 375°F.

Mix the oats, flour, and baking powder in a mixing bowl. Melt the margarine and stir this into the mixture. Slowly add a little boiling water, until you have a workable dough.

Knead gently on a floured surface until the dough is pliable and soft. Roll out to a thickness of about ⅛ inch. Cut out 18 rounds using a cookie cutter and put on a nonstick baking sheet.

Bake 10–15 minutes.

Note: triangles are a traditional oatcake shape, so roll the dough into two or three rounds and cut these across to make triangular wedges, if you prefer.

OPPOSITE: Apricot and Brandy Spread

FRUIT COMPOTE

You can vary the fruits in this to suit yourself. If the compote is going to be served within a day or so you can even add fresh fruits for a change.

Calories per serving: 248
Saturated fat: Low
Total fat: Low
Protein: Low
Carbohydrate: High
Cholesterol: None
Vitamins: Folic acid
Minerals: Iron, Potassium

2 ounces each dried pears and pitted prunes
3½ ounces each dried peaches and apple rings
1 ounce each dried banana flakes
2 tbsp golden raisins
1½ cups orange juice
3 whole cloves
1 small piece of cinnamon stick
1 tsp grated lemon zest
pinch of ground ginger

Place all the ingredients in a saucepan with ½ cup water, bring to a simmer, and cook until all the fruits are very tender (this varies greatly, so check after 20 minutes).
   Serve hot or cold.
Note: this will keep several days, covered, in the refrigerator.

GRANOLA

This granola is higher in fat and calories than muesli, but it is delicious sprinkled on yogurt and fruits or used as a topping for a fruit crisp.

Makes twelve 1-ounce servings
Calories per serving: 124
Saturated fat: Low
Total fat: High
Protein: Medium
Carbohydrate: Medium
Cholesterol: None
Vitamins: Folic acid, E
Minerals: Iron, Potassium

1 tbsp sunflower oil
2 tsp clear honey
2 cups rolled oats
⅓ cup wholewheat flakes
2 tbsp sesame seeds
2 tbsp sunflower seeds
¼ cup mixed chopped nuts
1 tsp ground cinnamon

Preheat the oven to 325°F.
Combine the oil and honey and mix with the other ingredients. Spread this out evenly on a nonstick baking sheet and bake about 30 minutes, turning once. Check regularly to ensure it isn't over-browning.
   Remove from the oven when deep golden brown.

SPECIAL RECIPE MUESLI

Makes eight 3-ounce servings
Calories per serving: 297
Saturated fat: Low
Total fat: Medium
Protein: Medium
Carbohydrate: High
Cholesterol: None
Vitamins: E, B group
Minerals: Iron, Calcium, Potassium, Magnesium

4 cups rolled oats, or mixture of rolled grains of choice
⅔ cup crushed bran flakes
⅓ cup each raisins, chopped dried apricots, and chopped dried peaches
3 tbsp each sunflower seeds, hazelnuts, and cashew nuts
2½ tbsp each chopped dates and wheatgerm
1½ tbsp sesame seeds

Mix all ingredients in a large bowl and store in an airtight container.
Note: you can vary the proportions – and, indeed, the types of nuts and fruits – to suit yourself, but bear in mind that if you increase the nut and seed content significantly you will also increase the fat and calorie content.

Basic recipes

Of course you can go out and buy all the basics you need for your cooking – from yogurt to pizza dough and pastry. Usually, however, it is healthier – and more fun – to make your own!

From time to time, everyone falls back on buying "basics." As we are all so busy, this is nothing to feel ashamed about. There are some highly acceptable basics on the market, from ready-made tomato sauces and mayonnaise to pastas.

There are, in fact, a few basics that are hardly worth the bother of making yourself. Bread-making, for example, is quite time-consuming and not everyone seems to have the gift for it – so why worry, when nowadays there is such a plentiful and varied supply of good breads in most areas – from Mediterranean varieties to organic loaves.

There are, however, some things that do seem always to taste better if you make them yourself. For instance, it is hard to get good wholewheat piecrust dough or crêpes; good vegetable stock is rare, and so is a good spice blend for curry.

Other ready-made products may seem quite acceptable, but they often have a high additive content. So I've selected several basic recipes that I think you will find most useful. I've included yogurt because, although you can find good yogurt in the stores, if – like me – you eat a lot of it, it can work out to be quite expensive. It is easy, quick, and inexpensive to make your own.

Crêpes, piecrust, and pizza dough can all be frozen, as can the vegetable stock (reduce it first to save storage space). The curry blend will keep a while in an opaque airtight jar, or in a glass jar in cool, dark conditions.

Dressings will keep a few days in the refrigerator. You can use the basic dressing recipes with your own variations – added spices and herbs, etc. You can also make a very simple dressing by mixing plain yogurt with lemon juice and seasonings. Most commercial dressings are quite high in fat, so it really is worth having a good repertoire that you can produce at home in a few shakes.

Pizza Dough (page 121); Wholewheat Piecrust Dough (page 120)   119

WHOLEWHEAT PIECRUST DOUGH

This quantity makes enough for an 8-inch quiche or tart to serve four.

Calories per serving: 145
Saturated fat: High
Total fat: High
Protein: Medium
Carbohydrate: Medium
Cholesterol: Not known
Vitamins: Folic acid, A, D
Minerals: Iron, Potassium

⅔ cup wholewheat flour
½ tsp baking powder
pinch of salt
¼ cup lowfat vegetable shortening
2–3 tbsp cold water

Sift the flour, baking powder, and salt into a mixing bowl, adding any flour left in the sifter to the bowl.

Put the shortening into the mixing bowl and cut it into the flour until the mixture resembles bread crumbs.

Sprinkle on 2 tablespoons of the cold water and draw the dough together with a spatula, adding a little more water if necessary until the dough comes away cleanly from the sides of the bowl. (Whatever you do, don't add too much water or you will spoil the pastry.)

Cover the bowl with foil and let it sit in the refrigerator for 30 minutes.

Lightly flour a pastry board or suitable surface and the rolling pin. Shape the dough into a flattish, even round and roll it out evenly and carefully, giving it a one-quarter turn or so between rollings, until you have a very thin sheet.

(If at any time the dough seems to be sticking to the board, lift it using the rolling pin and add more flour underneath and more flour to the rolling pin. If the dough splits, just stick it back together!)

Trim the dough to size before using it to line or cover the pan or pie. (To prevent the dough breaking, lift it using the rolling pin.)

EGG PASTA

Making pasta is quite easy, but my homemade version is not suitable for vegans as I find a homemade version without eggs is always disappointing.

Makes 4 very generous servings
Calories per serving: 360
Saturated fat: Low
Total fat: Low
Protein: Medium
Carbohydrate: High
Cholesterol: 187 mg
Vitamins: A, B group, D, E
Minerals: Calcium, Iron

2 cups + 2 tbsp flour
⅛ tsp salt
3 medium eggs
2 tsp olive oil

Make sure your work surface is very clean and dry. Put the flour on the surface. Sprinkle in the salt.

Make a well in the center and break the eggs into it. Pour in the oil and, using your fingers, gradually work the eggs and flour together until you have a dough.

Knead the dough until it is soft, pliable, and smooth, about 10 minutes. Roll it out as thinly as you can and then cut it into thin ribbons.

Cook the pasta in plenty of boiling salted water for about 3 minutes.

PIZZA DOUGH

You can buy ready-made pizza dough and some are quite good, but if you have a few spare minutes it is fun to make your own. You can make the dough using wholewheat flour. You can also put an egg into the mixture for a richer dough, but I prefer the non-egg version.

Calories per serving: 315
   (one-quarter of the base)
Saturated fat: Low
Total fat: Low
Protein: Medium
Carbohydrate: High
Cholesterol: None
Vitamins: Trace
Minerals: Calcium

2 cups + 2 tbsp flour
1 tsp salt
1 tsp active dry yeast
¾ cup hot water (hot to the touch)
1 tbsp olive oil

Sift the flour and salt into a large bowl. In a small bowl, whisk the yeast with a little of the water. Let stand until frothy, and then pour into the large bowl with the remaining water and oil.

Mix to a soft dough, adding a little more water if necessary, until the dough comes away cleanly from the bowl.

Knead the dough on a lightly floured surface for about 10 minutes. Place in a lightly oiled bowl, cover, and let rise in a warm place until doubled in size, about 45 minutes.

Oil a 12-inch pizza pan and press the dough in it to fit. Add a half quantity (or as much as you can get on) of Tomato Sauce (see page 69) plus your favorite topping, and bake in an oven preheated to 400°F for 25 minutes. *Note*: if you don't have a pizza pan you can shape the pizza on a baking sheet.

CRÊPES

∗ *Fill with lightly cooked asparagus spears and top with* Cheese Sauce *(page 67).*
∗ *Fill with the* Crispy Vegetable Pie *filling (page 86) and grate cheese over the top before baking.*
∗ *Fill sweet crêpes with chopped banana and brown sugar and top with puréed raspberries or apricots.*

Makes 8
Calories per serving (2 crêpes):
   157
Saturated fat: Low
Total fat: Medium
Protein: High
Carbohydrate: High
Cholesterol: 63 mg
Vitamins: A, B, D, E
Minerals: Calcium, Iron

⅔ cup + 1 tbsp all-purpose flour (or use wholewheat, or a mixture of equal parts buckwheat and wholewheat for French crêpes)
pinch of salt
1 medium egg
1 cup skim milk
little sugar to taste (for sweet crêpes)
2 tsp corn oil

Sift the flour and salt into a mixing bowl. Make a well in the center and add the egg. Gradually beat it in with little bits of the flour. Gradually add the milk as you do this and beat until you have a smooth batter. (You could do all this in a blender.) Add sugar, if using.

You can let the batter stand until you are ready to use it; it won't harm it.

When ready to make the crêpes, brush the bottom of a small nonstick frying pan with a little of the oil (which you should put in a saucer) and heat the pan well until you can feel the heat coming off the bottom.

Pour in just enough batter to coat the bottom and swirl around to make a thin crêpe. Cook until the base is golden (slip a spatula under to see), then turn and cook the other side for 30 seconds.

Transfer to a warm plate and keep warm, if necessary, while you make the rest.

Fill the crêpes as desired (see left).

VEGETABLE STOCK

This stock will form the basis of many soups and casseroles and is added to many other dishes, too. It is worth the effort of making it, as good ready-made stock is hard to find and bouillon cubes are not always too good.

Calories for the whole amount: about 75
Saturated fat: Low
Total fat: Low
Protein: Low
Carbohydrate: High
Cholesterol: None
Vitamins: C
Minerals: Potassium

1 large onion
2 medium carrots
2 large celery stalks
1 large leek
1 green bell pepper, seeded
fresh thyme
fresh parsley
12 black peppercorns
pared zest of 1 lemon

Chop the vegetables coarsely and put them in a saucepan with all the other ingredients and 1 quart of water.

Bring to a boil and skim the top, if necessary. Cover and simmer 45 minutes. Let cool slightly, then strain, pressing the vegetables to extract as much of the flavor and goodness as you can.

Store in the refrigerator and use as needed. It will keep a few days, or will freeze.

* Don't use potatoes or cabbage in stock, but you can use vegetables other than the ones listed – experiment and see how you do.
* You can reduce the strained stock for a fuller flavor by simmering, uncovered, until it is the strength you require.
* Don't add salt because not all recipes require a salted stock. Also, you may want to reduce the stock, and you can always add salt later.

CURRY POWDER

Calories per tablespoon: approximately 10
Saturated fat: Low
Total fat: Low
Protein: Low
Carbohydrate: High
Cholesterol: None
Vitamins: Trace
Minerals: Iron

1 tbsp cardamom pods
1 tbsp dried red chili pepper, seeded
1 tbsp cloves
½ cup coriander seeds
1 tbsp black peppercorns
1 tbsp ground ginger (ground yourself from a piece of dried gingerroot)
⅔ cup ground turmeric

First get the seeds out of the cardamom pods, using a rolling pin to crush the pods. Then grind each of the whole items individually in a small spice mill. Thoroughly mix together all the ingredients and use as required. It will keep quite well in an airtight jar for a couple of months before beginning to lose its bite.
Note: this makes a rich – but not too hot – curry; for a hotter powder, include the chili seeds.

YOGURT

Serves 4
Calories per 5 fl oz serving: 67
Saturated fat: Low
Total fat: Low
Protein: High
Carbohydrate: Medium
Cholesterol: 4 mg
Vitamins: Niacin, A
Minerals: Calcium

2 tbsp nonfat dry milk
2½ cups skim milk
1 tbsp plain yogurt with active live cultures.

Dissolve the milk powder in the milk and simmer a few minutes. Pour into a heatproof bowl and let cool to just warm. Add the yogurt and stir well. Pour into a wide-necked thermos and leave in a warm place for 5–6 hours.

When set, pour off and discard the whey that will be on top, and put the yogurt in the refrigerator.
Note: the fresher your yogurt starter, the better the result – if you use old yogurt you may get a bitter taste. Also, don't leave the yogurt in the thermos longer than is necessary for it to set.

OPPOSITE: Vegetable Stock ingredients

LIGHT MAYONNAISE

This is a perfectly acceptable mayonnaise-style dressing, which has only one-quarter of the calories of traditional mayonnaise. You will probably also find its lighter, tangier taste preferable in salads.

Makes ½ cup
Calories per level tbsp: 25
Saturated fat: Medium
Total fat: High
Protein: Medium
Carbohydrate: Low
Cholesterol: 10 mg per level tbsp
Vitamins: Trace
Minerals: Trace

2 heaping tbsp plain lowfat yogurt
3 tbsp reduced-calorie mayonnaise
2 tsp fresh lemon juice
pinch of dry mustard powder or
   turmeric
salt and black pepper

Blend all the ingredients together in a small bowl.

Stored in a jar in the refrigerator, it will keep for at least a week.
Variations: for a sweeter taste, add a pinch of sugar; for a seafood dressing, add tomato paste and paprika; for a spicy dressing, add 1 tablespoon of curry powder; for a green dressing, add 1 teaspoon or more of chopped fresh leafy herbs, such as parsley, chives, or chervil.

TOFU MAYONNAISE

This mayonnaise-style dressing is useful for vegans and is quite creamy and delicious.

Makes ⅓ cup
Calories per tbsp: 35
Saturated fat: High
Total fat: High
Protein: Medium
Carbohydrate: Low
Cholesterol: None
Vitamins: E
Minerals: Calcium

2 ounces silken tofu
1 tbsp sunflower oil
½ tsp Dijon mustard
1 tsp lemon juice
black pepper

Put all the ingredients except the pepper in the blender and blend. Add some pepper to taste and pour into a small lidded container.

Refrigerated, it will keep for a few days.
Variations: add garlic purée for more bite; add a pinch of saffron powder soaked in a tiny drop of water for a more Mediterranean-style dressing; add a few drops of Tabasco or other hot pepper sauce for a Mexican dip.

LIGHT VINAIGRETTE

Makes about 7 fl oz
Calories per tbsp: 71
Saturated fat: High
Total fat: High
Protein: Trace
Carbohydrate: Trace
Cholesterol: None
Vitamins: Trace
Minerals: Trace

½ cup extra virgin olive oil
2 tbsp red or white wine vinegar
1 garlic clove, minced
1 tbsp Dijon mustard
3 tbsp cold water
salt and black pepper

Put all the ingredients in a jar and shake well or mix in a blender.

Always shake this dressing well before use. Keep it in a covered bottle in the refrigerator and use within 1 month.
Note: if desired, add fresh herbs, such as a tablespoon of chopped tarragon, thyme, or rosemary.

OIL-FREE VINEGAR DRESSING

6 parts water
2 parts white wine vinegar
1 part balsamic vinegar
salt and black pepper

Blend all the ingredients together.

You can add herbs, garlic, or mustard to this dressing to vary its flavor.

Note: this tangy dressing is good with all leaf salads.

JUICE DRESSING

This makes a nice change from vinaigrette on all kinds of salads, and it also makes a good marinade – e.g. for tofu – particularly with the addition of spices.

Makes enough for 4
Calories per serving: 64
Saturated fat: High
Total fat: High
Protein: Trace
Carbohydrate: Low
Cholesterol: None
Vitamins: C, E
Minerals: Trace

2 tbsp extra virgin olive oil
1 tbsp each fresh orange, lemon, and
    lime juices
salt and black pepper

Put all the ingredients in a jar or blender and combine well.

Refrigerate in an airtight jar or bottle until needed.

Variations: add 2 teaspoons light soy sauce, or a piece of crushed peeled fresh gingerroot, or a dash of hot pepper sauce.

HOME-DRIED TOMATOES

As I use sun-dried tomatoes in oil quite a lot as a flavoring ingredient, I thought it would be useful to give you a recipe for making something like it yourself at home. They are particularly delicious on pizzas.

Total calories: 200
Saturated fat: Low
Total fat: Low
Protein: Trace
Carbohydrate: High
Cholesterol: None
Vitamins: A, C, E
Minerals: Potassium

2 pounds ripe plum tomatoes
2 tsp olive oil
salt
2 or 3 pinches of dried oregano

Preheat the oven to 300°F and lightly grease some baking sheets with the oil.

Cut the tomatoes into quarters and remove the central flesh and seeds.

Arrange the tomato quarters hollow-side up on the baking sheets and sprinkle with the salt and oregano. Dry in the oven for about 50 minutes to 1 hour.

Let cool and use as they are, or store in a jar of olive oil.

Index

Page numbers in *italic* refer to the photographs

CONVERSION CHART

For most general purposes the term "calorie" is used for the kilocalorie and this is the practice used throughout this book

CALORIES (kcal)	KILOJOULES (kJ)
1	4.18
50	210
100	420
150	630
200	835
250	1,045
300	1,255
400	1,670
500	2,090
600	2,510
750	3,135
1,000	4,180
1,100	4,560
1,200	5,015
1,300	5,435
1,400	5,850
1,500	6,270
1,600	6,690
1,700	7,105
1,800	7,525
1,900	7,940
2,000	8,360
2,100	8,780
2,250	9,405
2,500	10,450